Praise from Forward-Thinking Professionals

"In a world where buzzword fatigue and PowerPoint malaise are quickly making complexity the enemy, the Zaltmans offer us a road toward simplicity. Metaphors are not just artifacts of rhetoric, but essential signposts of meaning—and meaning, after all, is what brand marketers are trying to create."
> —Ted McConnell, Director of Digital Marketing Innovation, Procter & Gamble

"Metaphors can serve as powerful tools to communicate ideas creatively, but as Zaltman and Zaltman prove in this book, the true power of metaphors may lie in their ability to provoke deep and imaginative thinking. This book shows us that metaphors, when used well and appropriately, can help develop ideas in new and unexpected ways that can expand the boundaries of knowledge and practice."
> —Anil Menon, Vice President, Marketing and Strategy, IBM

"The Zaltmans' groundbreaking work introduces us to the deep metaphors that capture the universals of human thought and decision making irrespective of culture or nationality. This book is an indispensable guide for business leaders seeking to expand beyond traditional markets and benefit from the untapped potential of the four billion customers and wealth creators who are just entering the global economy."
> —Djordjija Petkoski, Head, Business, Competitiveness, and Development Team, World Bank Institute, The World Bank

"A huge challenge in marketing is to find positioning ideas that work globally. *Marketing Metaphoria* unlocks the door to the universal ideas that run our lives and is invaluable for those who aspire for their brands to have true meaning in people's lives."
> —Keith Pardy, Senior Vice President, Nokia Strategic Marketing

"Step into the land of *Marketing Metaphoria*, a world where consumers use just a few deep metaphors to organize the complexity of their daily lives. This book changed how *I* think about how *consumers* think. A must-read for anyone wanting a deep understanding of how consumers develop emotional connections to a brand."
> —Olin Hoover, Vice President, Consumer and Customer Insights, Pepperidge Farm, Inc.

"In today's market, companies cannot succeed without actionable insight into consumers' minds: how they interpret stimulus, how they make decisions. That's what makes *Marketing Metaphoria* a must-read. It sheds light on how to blend the science of the human condition with the discipline of brand management."
> —Mark Hendrix, Executive Vice President, Director of Corporate Marketing, The PNC Financial Services Group

"*Marketing Metaphoria* affirms that deeply held human needs and emotions are often not easily articulated. The authors clearly demonstrate how metaphors provide a window to the way consumers view not only products and services but the world around them."
> —Bernard D. Novgorodoff, PhD, AVP, Director, Consumer Insights Group, Brown-Forman Beverages

"Once again, the Zaltmans have given us tools to overcome the 'depth deficit' in corporate America! *Marketing Metaphoria* provides a fascinating and practical way to understand how to communicate to customers about the deep emotional benefits of products and services."

 —Jane Clarke, Vice President, Insights and Innovation, Time Warner
  Global Media Group

"With *Marketing Metaphoria*, the Zaltmans continue to challenge marketers to truly understand their customers at a deeper, more meaningful level. While acknowledging the complexity of this endeavor, they effectively use real-world examples to illustrate how the understanding of deep metaphors can be successfully applied to marketing strategy and execution. Their perspectives on segmentation and traditional interview methods are particularly refreshing in a field that has seen little innovation. The Zaltmans continue to excite and inspire me with *Marketing Metaphoria*!"

 —Marc White Sr., Insight Director, Global Marketing,
  AstraZeneca Pharmaceuticals

"This book provides an approach to building global love for brands by positioning emotional benefit within engaging communication. The Deep Metaphor framework provides the common thread, giving global brands local relevance."

 —Eapen George, Vice President, Flavor Development and Innovation,
  PepsiCo, International

"In a business world long on data and short on meaning, the Zaltmans' deep metaphors provide powerful lenses through which to understand customers deeply and translate such understanding into action. By turns brilliantly insightful and pragmatically prescriptive, this book is a formidable competitive weapon for marketers and strategists alike."

 —Jeffrey F. Rayport, Chairman of Marketspace LLC,
  a Monitor Group company

"Fascinating! This book helps you understand why traditional research techniques have such a low batting average, and provides a road map for understanding the true motivators of consumer action. It will surely help its readers overcome the 'depth deficit' in thinking and set them on their way to deeper thinking and deeper profits."

 —Michael Wendroff, Vice President, Marketing, Combe, Inc.

"The Zaltmans' book will be transformational for marketers who learn to listen carefully for the 'invisible piper' inside their target audiences, and for anyone engaged in important global activity—be it business, government, or politics—who will learn that success springs from understanding the things that unite us."

 —Robert Barocci, President and CEO,
  The Advertising Research Foundation

"A welcome antidote to the superficiality that afflicts too many books on consumer psychology. Where others focus on trivial differences between market segments, the Zaltmans explore the deeply rooted beliefs spanning eras and cultures that frame our comprehension of marketing messages. The result is a book that is readable, insightful, and very, very human."

 —Scott McDonald, Senior Vice President, Market Research,
  Condé Nast Publications

"This fantastic book is an indispensable next step in deeper thinking, one that should be adopted by all those who are interested in effective communication in every area of life—be it marketing, managing people, or even personal relationships."

> —Tadeusz Żórawski, President, Universal McCann Poland

"The only book of its kind that provides a breakthrough framework for a deeper understanding of creating greater value and more meaningful experiences for customers."

> —Lou Carbone, author and founder and Chief Experience Officer, Experience Engineering, Inc.

Praise from Renowned Business Scholars

"After reading this beautifully written and compelling book, you will understand consumers—and yourself—better than you ever have before."

> —Leonard Berry, M. B. Zale Chair in Retailing and Marketing Leadership, Mays Business School, Texas A&M University

"The Zaltman team takes us behind the scenes to probe deeply into the emotional drivers of consumer behavior. When armed with their insights you will surely think differently about how to make your products more relevant and your communications more compelling."

> —George S. Day, Geoffrey T. Boisi Professor, Wharton School, University of Pennsylvania

"This mind-bender of a milestone reminds me of Carl Jung on archetypes and Noam Chomsky on linguistics and language formation. You will never think the same again about what shapes consumer behavior, thanks to this eye-opening book."

> —Philip Kotler, S. C. Johnson & Son Distinguished Professor of International Marketing, Kellogg School of Management, Northwestern University

"In this wonderful guide to how consumers think, the authors' research reveals seven basic metaphors that underlie consumer behavior across seemingly diverse groups. Anyone wedded to traditional market research methods or interested in emotions and unconscious thought will benefit from reading this engaging book."

> —Don Lehmann, George E. Warren Professor of Business, Columbia Business School

"This book provides the answer to the oft-quoted paradox: 'If companies only knew what they know.' In Toyota, deep metaphors are part of what it calls the 'nerve system' of communication. Deep metaphors are the key to communicating tacit knowledge in today's knowledge-driven society."

> —Hirotaka Takeuchi, dean of the business school at Hitotsubashi University and coauthor, *Extreme Toyota* (forthcoming)

MARKETING
METAPHORIA

Also by Gerald Zaltman

How Customers Think

Essential Insights into the Mind of the Market

Gerald Zaltman

Hearing the Voice of the Market

Competitive Advantage Through Creative
Use of Market Information

Vincent Barabba and Gerald Zaltman

MARKETING METAPHORIA

WHAT DEEP METAPHORS
REVEAL ABOUT THE MINDS
OF CONSUMERS

GERALD ZALTMAN

LINDSAY H. ZALTMAN

Harvard Business Press

Boston, Massachusetts

Printed in the United States of America

12 11 10 09 08   5 4 3 2 1

Library of Congress Cataloging-in-Publication Data

Zaltman, Gerald.
    Marketing metaphoria : what seven deep metaphors reveal about the minds of consumers / Gerald Zaltman, Lindsay H. Zaltman.
        p. cm.
    Includes bibliographical references and index.
    ISBN 978-1-4221-2115-3
        1. Consumer behavior. 2. Metaphor. I. Zaltman, Lindsay H. II. Title.
    HF5415.32.Z353 2008
    658.8'342—dc22

                                                    2007040116

The paper used in this publication meets the requirements of the American National Standard for Permanence of Paper for Publications and Documents in Libraries and Archives Z39.48-1992.

Human beings, vegetables, or cosmic dust—
we all dance to a mysterious tune, intoned
in the distance by an invisible piper.

—Albert Einstein

Metaphor is so widespread in language that
it's hard to find expressions for
abstract ideas that are not *metaphorical.*

—Stephen Pinker,
The Stuff of Thought

Contents

Undressing the Mind
of the Consumer:
Introduction to Deep Metaphors

Not long ago, "Jenny," a twenty-year-old bookkeeper for a small building contractor, agreed to share her thoughts and feelings about becoming a first-time mother. To prepare for our meeting, we asked her to collect eight images, clipped from magazines and other sources, that represented how she felt about this phase of her life.

Every day around the globe, we and our global licensee-partners interview people like Jenny in depth, on behalf of many of the world's most respected firms, leading brands, and non-profit organizations, all of which need a deeper understanding of the topic at hand. We use a special interview approach developed because most of what people know, they do not know that they know—and what they say may not be what they mean—since most thoughts and other important cognitive processes occur unconsciously. Consequently, people cannot readily articulate many important thoughts and feelings unless we go beyond the typical survey or focus group to help them do so.

For the first ninety minutes of this new mother's visit, our interviewer asked her to discuss each picture. The special interviewing techniques used help surface important, often hidden thoughts and feelings. The interviewer also asked her to imagine and describe a one-act play or short movie involving particular characters relevant to new motherhood. The interview yielded almost twenty-five pages of single-spaced text capturing the verbalizations, chuckles, sighs, pauses, and other indications of the emotions the new mother experienced as she described these recent, life-changing events—all very important to the sponsor of this research, a global leader in products designed for children. Like many of our clients, this company sought to overcome what we call a *depth deficit*, a lack of careful reflection and bold thinking about rich consumer information. The company understood that it needed more insight into the larger context—the emotional experiences of being a new parent—that made its products relevant. Depth deficits in managerial thinking are characterized by several shortcomings:

- A failure to probe beneath consumers' own surface thinking

- A failure to use insights from different disciplines to formulate research issues and to interpret relevant data

- An absence of bold, imaginative thinking about what can engage a consumer's mind

Deep deficits in thinking reveal themselves in weak product and service development, low-impact marketing communications, and ineffective product-launch strategies. The deficits are widespread across industries—in fact, approximately 60 to 80 percent of new products fail in their first year, and more fail soon thereafter. Furthermore, many established products fail to reach new markets or fail to increase consumption among current customers. For these reasons, remedying this deficiency is arguably the single largest challenge facing corporate leaders today.[1] For our clients, the best way to meet that challenge is to get inside the hearts and minds of consumers and understand how they really think. Our two-hour individual interviews do just that.

During the second part of the new mother's visit, we introduced her to Mark, one of our digital imagers, a specially trained graphic artist who scans a participant's images into a computer just before the interview. She sat down next to him at his computer and walked him through her eight images. He asked, "Which image is most important to you? What is the most important idea?"

"Mmmm," Jenny said, pointing to the picture of a pinkish red lily in nearly full bloom. "This blossom is new and represents our daughter. She is so new and innocent and pure. She is growing quickly and is really, really beautiful. My husband and I have given birth to this amazing little flower."

"How important is this idea of giving birth to your daughter?" Mark asked. "How large or small should this idea be in your collage?"

"With respect to being a new parent, it is everything," she said. "It should be as large as you can make it."

Mark changed the size of the flower image on screen using Photoshop software. "Like that?"

She nodded, pleased. "Yes, the flower is covering the entire canvas."

"What would be the next most important idea?" he asked.

"Not the vase, I don't think. It would be either . . . ," Jenny hesitated, her hand fluttering over the pictures on the desk. "Either the elephant or the necklace. Go with the necklace."

Mark moved the image of the pearl necklace on top of the first image on screen. To her, the necklace represented the circle of life. She wanted the necklace fairly large, since the idea of the circle of life was nearly as important as the flower.

When Mark asked about the relationship between the circle of life and the flower, she said, "I think the degree to which I love and cherish my daughter depends upon how I feel connected to the circle of life. Sometimes I wonder whether I will be a good mother, but that doubt quickly leaves when I think about how important the circle of life is and how vital a role I play in it."

"How might we visually represent that relationship?" he asked.

She knew immediately. "The flower should be emerging from the necklace, protected and nurtured by that ring of pearls. In fact, can we use the vase now? I think the vase is important because it is really about the shape of childhood. She has her own personality, her own shape."

He made the flower smaller, more delicate; the vase returned to surround the flower, and the necklace was placed in a circle around both. He then asked her about the next most important idea, and the next, each time asking Jenny to tell him something about what the idea represented and its role in the larger conversation, or "picture." In addition to the flower and the necklace, she brought images of an elephant, a clock, a diamond, a bathtub, and a juggler. Mark patiently arranged and rearranged the images on the screen, enlarging, reducing, bringing something to the foreground or background, adding color, and generally doing whatever was necessary to create a collage according to Jenny's specifications. He was in essence serving as Jenny's hands while implementing her thoughts. When they finished the collage, the pearl necklace encircled everything but the juggler and the bathtub.

As the final stage, we asked Jenny to explain the image she created (figure I-1 in color insert). She titled her collage "Coming Full Circle" for this reason: "Our family and I have changed so much. We have this new life, but we are part of something much bigger than our little family."

Nearly all the interviews we conducted on becoming a first-time mother revealed the same unconscious viewing lenses—specifically, those of transformation, connection, and container—which shape many new mothers' experiences as consumers. We call these lenses *deep metaphors*, that is, metaphors that structure what we think, hear, say, and do. Deep metaphors are enduring ways of perceiving things, making sense of what we encounter, and guiding our subsequent actions. Put differently, deep metaphors are the product of an ever-evolving partnership between brain, body, and society. They populate the land of Metaphoria, a place where our basic views of the world are formed. Insights about the nature of these deep metaphors with respect to parenthood in Jenny's project provided significant direction in finding new product ideas, how to position new and existing products, and how to develop engaging product communications with new parents.

Deep metaphors do matter, as we will see throughout this book. For instance, a senior manager at Procter & Gamble reports that the company's attentiveness to deep metaphors doubled the first-year sales of Febreze over prelaunch estimates.

The result was the most successful new product in P&G history at the time.[2]

Deep metaphors start developing at birth and are shaped by our social environment. In this sense, they are innate capacities or propensities, as are other capacities such as those for language, emotion, and three-dimensional vision.[3] They are *deep* because they operate largely unconsciously. They are *metaphors* because they re-present, or play around with, nearly everything we encounter.[4] They unconsciously add, delete, and distort information while continuously giving us the impression that we engage our world exactly as it is.

Equally important, deep metaphors capture what anthropologists, psychologists, and sociologists call *human universals*, or near universals, the traits and behaviors found in nearly all societies.[5] That is, people from very different backgrounds and different parts of the world use the same relatively few deep metaphors. Our interviews are designed to uncover deep metaphors.

Three Levels of Metaphorical Thinking

People usually define a metaphor as the representation of one thing in terms of something else. This book uses *metaphor* more broadly as shorthand for many forms of idiomatic, nonliteral expressions or representations. In addition to deep metaphors, there are two other relevant levels of metaphors at work.

Surface metaphors are those that we use in everyday language, such as "This problem is just the tip of the iceberg," "Planning for my golden years is an uphill, rocky road," or "Let's consider this issue water under the bridge." Across many languages, people spontaneously use about five to six metaphors per minute in spoken conversation. These metaphors are meaningful by themselves, but are also jumping-off points for probing deeper thoughts and feelings.

Metaphor themes reside below surface metaphors, but are not completely buried in our unconscious. As the common dimension underlying similar surface metaphors, the themes are important for marketers. Metaphor themes reflect the more basic viewing lens we call deep metaphors.

Figure I-1 illustrates the different metaphor levels. Surface metaphors or everyday expressions such as "Money runs through his fingers," "I am drowning in debt," "Don't pour your money down the drain," and "The bank froze his assets" suggest a metaphor theme that says money is like a liquid. This theme, in turn, reflects the deep metaphor of resource.

Across people and settings, there is variation, of course, in how the same deep metaphors operate and manifest themselves. But to know whether and how to leverage these variations or which to stress when multiple deep metaphors are in play, you must first identify deep metaphors and appreciate how they

FIGURE I-1

Money is like liquid

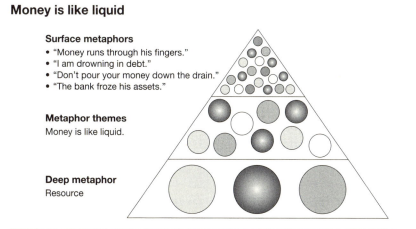

Surface metaphors
- "Money runs through his fingers."
- "I am drowning in debt."
- "Don't pour your money down the drain."
- "The bank froze his assets."

Metaphor themes
Money is like liquid.

Deep metaphor
Resource

xviii   Undressing the Mind of the Consumer

play in our unconscious minds. Our mission is to help you gain that understanding.

Of course, our approach does not replace other validated research methods, especially those that lend themselves to quantitative analyses. All methods are compromises with reality. The challenge is finding the best method or set of methods for the problem at hand without recasting the problem so that it conforms to a comfortable, familiar method.

This book introduces not only the ideas that we and colleagues from several countries have developed about deep metaphors but also the multidisciplinary research that informs and supports these ideas. We use a disproportionate number of examples from Olson Zaltman Associates and its global licensee-partners because we can provide greater background and detail. Typically in our research, we apply the patented Zaltman Metaphor Elicitation Technique (ZMET), which consists of several steps during a one-on-one interview such as the one just described. Each step is based on well-documented facets of cognition and proven ways of understanding them.[6] While the basic steps are the same across projects, their actual implementation varies considerably, depending on the research topic and the decisions to make.

Our goal in this book, however, is not to train you in this research technique or describe it in detail; rather, it is to demonstrate that deep metaphors play powerfully yet silently in the unconscious minds of consumers, are relatively few, and are universal. You will see how we interpret consumers' surface expressions and imagery to detect their deep metaphors. You will also learn how managers leverage deep metaphors to evaluate and test new concepts, identify new product and service opportunities, and position new or existing products. Other uses for deep metaphors will be discussed: the evaluation of brand and corporate images, the development and evaluation of communications programs, and the design of better packaging and new physical environments. Deep metaphors have also yielded great insight into internal organizational issues, important social issues, and public policy matters.

The Journey Ahead

Chapter 1 identifies a deficit in deep thinking among managers and discusses some factors contributing to this deficit, particularly managers' tendencies to overemphasize surface-level differences among consumers and to neglect the deep metaphors that enable us to observe such differences in the first place. Deep metaphors loom large in the complex landscape that all managers must navigate: the consumer's unconscious mind. We argue that managers can use consumers' deep metaphors to overcome the depth deficit in their own thinking.

Chapter 2 briefly introduces some of the social, psychological, physical, and neurological bases for deep metaphors. Throughout the book, we provide more in-depth documentation in the endnotes, which serve as gateways to larger bodies of supporting evidence.

Chapters 3 through 9 address specific deep metaphors. Each chapter presents some of the scientific underpinnings for a particular deep metaphor as well as a set of commonly heard expressions—outcroppings of this deep metaphor—that consumers use in variations around the world. Each chapter gives examples of how real companies—some of which are necessarily disguised—have applied their understanding of a deep metaphor to address a particular business issue. In many cases, these companies have, understandably, asked us not to disclose the exact applications of the deep metaphors or a management team's thinking processes. Fortunately, this nondisclosure does not prevent our introducing the reader to deep metaphors, how consumers experience them, and how managers use them. To illustrate the presence of deep metaphors in consumer thinking, each chapter contains a digital image like Jenny's and a short excerpt of the interviewee's description. The digital image, however, represents only one of several ZMET steps used to uncover deep metaphors.

Chapter 10 details the use of deep metaphors and discusses how new thoughts and feelings emerge when multiple deep metaphors are surfacing around a topic. Finally, we provide examples from nonconsumer settings to illustrate the presence of deep metaphors in all corners of everyone's daily life.

As you read these chapters, you will make several discoveries:

- A given quote and an image may reveal more than one deep metaphor. In fact, most matters in life involve two or more deep metaphors. For this reason, we have deliberately reused certain examples in different chapters.

- Just because a topic seems to involve a specific deep metaphor—for example, vacation travel is a journey—does not mean that the idea of a journey is the primary deep metaphor at play in the minds of consumers. It could be transformation instead. Basically, a consumer's primary viewing lens depends on the facet of a topic being explored and its perspective.

- How marketers ask consumers to discuss a topic influences how consumers respond. When asked about planning a vacation, people may use the idea of a journey as the most relevant deep metaphor. When asked about benefiting from a vacation, they may speak of transformation rather than a journey.

- Consumers view different brands in the same category through the lens of different deep metaphors. For instance, Michelin invokes the deep metaphor of container (chapter 6), while Pirelli invokes control (chapter 9). Budweiser "owns" the deep metaphor of connection (chapter 7), and Coors owns the deep metaphors of force and nature.

- Different market segments may engage the same deep metaphor differently. Jenny felt good about the transformations of new motherhood, whereas others interviewed for this project experienced their transformations more negatively.

The book's epigraph nicely captures the spirit of *Marketing Metaphoria*: "Human beings, vegetables, or cosmic dust—we all dance to a mysterious tune, intoned in the distance by an invisible piper." We have no evidence that vegetables and cosmic dust dance to any tune, let alone a mysterious one, but we know that human beings do. In this book, the invisible piper is the unconscious mind, where most thought originates, and those mysterious tunes are deep metaphors. Each metaphor is complex and far-reaching, but not that mysterious, once you learn to listen carefully.

1

How to Think Deeply

A Brief Guide to Overcoming Your Depth Deficit

McCann-Erickson Worldwide, a global leader in marketing communications, wanted to understand the challenges that chief executive officers and chief marketing officers face in achieving top-line growth in their firms. To get at the core issues, we conducted a number of lengthy interviews with some of the world's most thoughtful and respected business leaders. For this book, we supplemented that initial study with additional interviews of leading industry executives so that our sample covered diverse industries.[1] So, what was their biggest challenge? Without exception, these executives pointed to the depth deficit within their companies. They spoke not only about the absence of careful, imaginative thinking but also about the significant cost of its absence. One executive told us:

*We do not have deep consumer insights . . . Just because my man-
agers consume the products and watch the focus groups, they think
they understand consumers. They do not. When I push them to explain a consumer insight that excites them, they often cannot. They
have not thought deeply about it. If it did not upset me so much, I
might feel sorry for them.*

Why Johnny Can't Think Deeply

Deep thinking is hard work. A senior officer at IBM told us he
counsels his managers with this advice: "Never confuse working
hard with thinking hard."[2] Managers do not think deeply simply by poring over memos and reports, participating in lots of
meetings and conference calls, and logging long hours at the
office or on the road. We think deeply by applying disciplined
imagination to deep insights from consumers.

Nearly every executive mentioned several factors that contribute to depth deficits: short-term thinking, outdated marketing knowledge, a discouraging work environment evidenced by
the lack of true managerial support and reward systems, the basic
fear of change, and the seduction of superficial differences.

The Lethal Impact of Short-Term Thinking

Executives commented at length on the negative consequences
of focusing on short-term results, or *presentism*. Thinking only
about the present or the near future leaves no mental bandwidth
for deep thinking. Two aspects of presentism surfaced in our
conversations: (1) a failure to consider what one does not know
and needs to learn, and (2) a desire to produce quick, short-term
results that occurs at the expense of thoughtfulness.

Lack of Genuine Managerial Support and Fear of Punishment

One popular excuse for not thinking deeply is "not enough time." Yes, you do need considerable time to think deeply and carefully, and managers do have many responsibilities that usurp that time. But if thinking deeply is so important, then why do companies not make time available? Even when they do, why do so few employees take advantage of it? Because, despite frequent managerial pronouncements about the need to take risks, company systems and processes do not authentically support employees' efforts.

One executive described an experiment in her previous company, where unit heads offered to make special arrangements for a select group of managers so that they had more time to think. The result? "Not one person opted to participate. That scared me. It spoke volumes about the future of that company. The need to avoid punishment trumped whatever rewards success would offer." She elaborated: "Everyone knew that despite what senior management said, the company punished failure by overlooking risk takers for promotion or refusing their budget increases."

When people lack experience in thinking deeply, are unclear about how thinking deeply differs from what they currently do, or have not observed anyone actually doing it well and getting rewarded in the organization, then they have little incentive to think deeply. They may fear that nothing better will result after incurring costs and absorbing risks.

Companies also discourage risk taking—where the risk is thinking differently and deeply—because it may be disruptive. Stephen Haeckel, executive trainer and consultant, explained it this way: "Institutionalized sense-making frameworks reward efficiency, not innovation. Innovation is disruptive and a natural enemy of efficiency, stability, and predictability."[3]

Fear of Change and the Unfamiliar

Implicit organizational norms are not the only impediments to deep thinking. A basic fear of thinking differently, partly rooted in the organizational climate, is another force. One CEO from an industrial products firm observed: "We have bright, energetic people in marketing. But for all their technical skills and hard work, they lack courage. They are afraid to think deeply. They fear the deep, I guess. Unfortunately, that is where the big fish swim, but they stick to the shallows and collect minnows."

We usually feel more comfortable "going with the flow" and thinking like everyone else in the organization. Fear of thinking differently is related to the psychological cost of changing one's mind. The technical term for this fear is *phonemophobia*, the fear of having new and unfamiliar thoughts appear, whether they are one's own thoughts or those of others. These thoughts may generate difficult emotions and uncomfortable feelings. By staying focused on familiar thoughts, a manager can avoid such negative experiences.

There is a related fear, *metathesiophobia*, the fear of change. Thinking differently may require behaving differently, which can be disruptive and threatening. For example, to think more deeply and imaginatively about data, a manager must allocate more time, abandon the comfort of outdated methods, and learn new, more scientifically grounded techniques.

Thinking deeply may involve changing how a manager defines, approaches, and acts on problems. For some managers, these changes can be deeply emotional and risky in terms of time, energy, uncertainty about outcomes, impact on self-esteem, and how one is viewed or treated by others.[4]

The Seduction of Differences

Even though they may fear differences in thinking, managers ironically spend substantial intellectual and financial resources addressing differences among consumers to identify market segments and differentiate products, strategies that can contribute to marketing success. However, marketers often focus on relatively inconsequential differences when segmenting markets and positioning products. Even though a difference may be statistically significant, it may be substantively inconsequential and unlikely to influence consumer behavior. An executive in one of the world's largest consumer products companies told us about the oversegmentation of a product category of considerable importance to his firm:

> *Six years ago, we spent millions of dollars devising a global market segmentation plan. We identified seven different segments in nine global regions. None of this was arbitrary: we had precise, reliable data about the distinctions among these segments. About a year ago, we finally figured out that our segmentation scheme had not substantially changed our top-line growth. This time around, our advertising agency really earned its fees. Its research demonstrated that there were really just three hot buttons for consumers and these varied somewhat globally. In effect, we were dealing with only three segments. That learning made a huge difference in turning us around. We had not seen the forest because of all the trees. We got seduced by differences.*

Managers must also understand the context of a measure of difference because context establishes its importance. Psychologist Jerome Kagan spoke of the importance of context: "The meaning of a single measure is as ambiguous as that of a verb lacking a noun or object . . . There is not one example in the history of the social sciences in which a particular measure had a single, unambiguous meaning—not one!"[5] Consider the precise physiological measures of particular brain activations. Biometrics can help us assess the presence or absence of negative and positive emotions. In one study, marketers used two physiological measures to test two alternative life insurance advertisements. Both measures indicated the presence of strong negative emotions in one advertisement and their relative absence in the other. Since both advertisements were designed to stimulate feelings of guilt, the managers assumed that the first advertisement achieved this goal more effectively.

But neither measure indicated conclusively that the advertisements were indeed stimulating guilt. They showed differences between the ads but not whether the consumers were feeling guilt, shame, remorse, embarrassment, or something else—all very different emotions. Knowing which emotion or emotions the consumers experienced would be critical in the marketing decision. Decision makers must understand the content of an emotion and not just whether an emotional state arose at all. The company decided to test both ads using a storytelling approach to learn what meanings the consumers coauthored or cocreated in each case.[6] The findings produced a modification of the second ad, which is proving very successful in engaging consumers.

Certainly, differences can be significant and have many practical implications for market strategies and tactics. But too often, marketers measure differences because they can. We certainly advocate precise measurements as long as they measure important things. However, just because we can devise a measure and obtain reliable responses about a trait or behavior does not make that measure important.[7] The advertising industry, for example, emphasizes the number of people exposed to an advertisement within a period, because marketers can measure that number readily and reliably. The industry devotes less attention to the more important but difficult measurement of whether an advertisement engages viewers constructively and has an enduring emotional impact—which is an advertisement's ultimate purpose.

Moreover, emphasizing differences distracts us with surface issues so that we lose insights into important drivers of consumer behavior. Focusing on similarities forces us to critique the underlying bases that we use when making distinctions. In the end, such examination improves our measures. In fact, we cannot make comparisons and draw distinctions, which are at the heart of segmenting markets and differentiating products, without referring to an underlying dimension that enables such contrasting observations. Distinctions have their roots in commonalities.

Finally, since similarities among people do not stand out as differences do, we underestimate the prevalence of similarities. Psychologist Daniel Gilbert notes, "Because if you are like most people, then like most people, you don't know you're like most people."[8] Psychologist Elizabeth Spelke, whose pioneering work is reshaping our understanding of human development, has commented similarly: "We have a tendency, when we think intuitively about ourselves and other people, to greatly overemphasize differences. We think that differences we can see on the surface signal some deeper, underlying difference, and I think this is almost always an illusion . . . We are deeply alike."[9]

Because we know ourselves better than we do others, we very much like the idea that we are unique, and we tend to overestimate how unique we really are. Similarly, because we know our group, society, and culture better than we understand others, we like to think it is unique and overestimate just how unique it really is. These biases cause marketing managers to overly focus on consumer differences and miss important commonalities among them. Ignoring alikeness as an important driver of thought and behavior leads to depth deficits in strategic thinking. We will return to this issue later.

Outdated Knowledge About How Customers Think

Most marketing practice is rooted in outdated or incomplete knowledge of how the mind works.[10] Since the mid-1980s, scientists have made remarkable advances in understanding why and how people think and act as they do.[11] Most managers are unaware of these developments because knowledge spreads slowly across disciplines. One executive noted:

> So often our consumer research is a dead weight to thinking instead of being a springboard for finding better ways of connecting with our markets. The problem is inadequate thinking, not inadequate data. What do I mean by inadequate thinking? [Managers] are using outdated models of human behavior. Now that I think of it, our data is probably inadequate for the same reasons.

For example, in surveys, marketers often ask consumers to respond to such statements as "Financial planning is difficult," "Chewing breath mints freshens my mouth," and "Going to the theater makes me happy." Companies want to know how much consumers agree with these statements, whether their responses vary by market segment, and whether significant changes in their responses have occurred over time. This information can help in identifying problems or assessing the effects of specific marketing activities.

But when consumers attach ratings of agreement and importance to such statements, the responses reveal only thoughts about what managers and researchers deem important but might not actually be the most relevant drivers of consumer behavior. In other words, consumers are responding to ideas imposed on them, not generated by them. Political psychologist Drew Westen, in his critique of focus groups, comments, "If you ask people conscious questions about unconscious processes, they will be happy to offer you their theories. But most of the time, those theories are wrong."[12]

Moreover, consumers may not really mean what they say. As noted psychologist and linguist Steven Pinker notes, "Words are not the same as thought [and] much of human wisdom consists of not mistaking one for the other."[13] Gaps between saying and meaning typically arise when consumers make nonroutine decisions, for example, when they respond to a new product or switch brands.[14] This constitutes the *say-mean gap*, which we will explore later in this chapter. Focusing only on the *say* (product attributes and functional benefits) produces surface-level managerial thinking. This level of thinking contributes to the depth deficit because managers fail to ask about the social and psychological consequences of those benefits (deeper thinking). Nor do they ask how those social or psychological consequences fit into a consumer's values, beliefs, and life goals (still deeper thinking). Brand battles are waged and won or lost at the deepest level.

The Joy of Workable Wondering

In our work, we have come to refer to the process of thinking deeply as *workable wondering*. Workable wondering involves the use of empirical, rigorous, and relevant information, also called workable knowledge, to challenge our assumptions and to engage in disciplined imagination.[15] It means more than collecting information. It means thinking deeply about the consumer insights that we have surfaced. It requires reading between the lines and detecting what else is present, well beyond what we already know.[16]

Several executives evaluate their staffs in terms of this ability. One told us, "It is not just the sense they make out of the information they have; it is how they add value by going beyond what they've got. That is what I look for. Do they dare to imagine?" Another executive said, "It is not what is in front of you that provides real competitive advantage. Competitors may have that, too. It is what you think that no else thinks to think, even when they have the same information."

Regarding their experiences in generating deep insights, every executive underscored the importance of contemplating that which is missing. An executive explained, "The 'Aha!' is in spotting the missing connection between the dots. It is there, but no one else sees it until you point it out." That is what happened when IBM brought out its first personal computer, and when Toyota introduced its Prius amid the craze for sports utility vehicles. Until those introductions, no one imagined a market. Without workable wondering, many of the goods and services we now take for granted would not exist. Someone had to engage in deep, disciplined, and imaginative thinking to see such possibilities as the need for personal computers, energy-efficient automobiles, cell phones, iPods, and gourmet coffee houses.

Most executives in our interviews felt they were making progress in encouraging workable wondering and overcoming the depth deficit. But it is clearly an uphill battle, one that requires commitment at the very top.[17] For example, Jeffrey R. Immelt, CEO of General Electric, has established a class of projects now well known as *imagination breakthroughs*. The projects consist of ideas that are "really hard or really important" and might generate significant revenues over a three-year period, the time that GE usually takes to implement a new idea. "Imagination breakthroughs are a protected class of ideas—safe from the budget slashers *because I've blessed each one*."[18] Immelt's strategy, which is succeeding, is to grow from a hundred such projects to a thousand by focusing more on imagination throughout the company. Immelt's innovation is to imagine beyond the short-term gain and to see future profits not driven solely by quarterly reports.

How Deep Metaphors Fuel Workable Wondering (and Bridge the Say-Mean Gap)

Obviously, the quality of a manager's thinking is closely linked to the quality of the information to think about. If deep insights from consumers are absent, then it matters little how imaginative the managers are. A key requirement, then, for workable wondering—that is, for thinking deeply and imaginatively *about* consumers—is having deep insights *from* consumers. Such insights come from (1) exploring beyond consumers' surface-level thinking and behavior into their unconscious mind, and (2) learning from *their* perspective *why* and *how* they think and do what they do.[19]

Deep metaphors can help us gain these insights. By probing and analyzing the nonliteral expressions of consumers' metaphors, we can compare what consumers are actually experiencing with what they are saying about the experience.[20] When given the right opportunity, consumers will usually reveal these hidden thoughts, regardless of background factors such as years of formal education. When consumers are empowered to explore their thinking and speak at length about a topic, their expressions become rich and revealing. Consider these examples:

- "Planning for my golden years is an uphill, rocky road" (forty-year-old American woman on financial planning).

- "Chewing breath mints is like throwing a party for your mouth" (fifty-two-year-old Frenchman discussing the benefits of breath mints).

- "When I go to the theater, I feel like a young girl again" (thirty-six-year-old Spanish American woman on the meaning of the arts in her life).

- "I'm stuck. Trapped. When I look at my future, I see more todays" (eighteen-year-old Macedonian man on his prospects in life).

- "If I eat pizza now, I just know I'll pay for it later" (twenty-three-year-old woman discussing heartburn).

Each statement is a figure of speech that suggests more than the idea that retirement planning is difficult or that chewing mints refreshes one's mouth.[21] For example, by exploring in one-on-one interviews phrases like "an uphill, rocky road," a financial services firm revealed additional ideas involving frustration, challenge, disappointment, hard work, and luck. When the company explored those thoughts further, it identified other important ideas to consider in its decision making. These deeper ideas are not available from survey responses to statements such as "financial planning is difficult" or in focus groups in which each participant has about ten minutes of airtime.

Figures of speech, then, often signal the presence of other ideas that tell a deeper, more meaningful story about consumers' experiences with goods and services than is revealed by direct questioning. Deep metaphors capture and reveal these deeper understandings, uncovered by probing, nondirective explorations of nonliteral or figurative surface expressions. For example, we found the following deep metaphors (in italics) in the studies that provided the preceding quotes:

- Financial planning is a *journey*.

- Breath mints are a *resource* for renewal.

- The arts *transform* one life stage to another.

- The here and now is a *container* that may have no opening or escape hatch for the future.

- Punishment will *balance out* the enjoyment of indiscreet eating.

In many ways, deep metaphors and emotions are siblings. Both are hardwired in our brains and shaped by social contexts and experiences. Moreover, deep metaphors and emotions are unconscious operations that are vital perceptual and cognitive functions. Finally, though they are few, deep metaphors and emotions are universal. That is, people experience them at the same basic level worldwide.

Of course, people vary in what triggers emotions such as fear, sadness, or joy and in how these emotions are expressed. Similarly, differences arise in how people experience a given deep metaphor. These differences are shaped by unique individual experiences and by social contexts, including the impact of a firm's marketing activities on consumers.[22] Consider two consumers commenting on financial planning. Both viewed financial planning as a journey. One, from a lower socioeconomic background than the person who described financial planning as a "rocky road," expressed the idea of a journey this way: "Birthdays, anniversaries, Christmas, and just plain old temptation are roadblocks to my putting money away for old age." Here, the idea is expressed of a journey thwarted by tempting detours, whereas the other consumer stressed the plain hardship of the journey.

Deep metaphors and emotions work hand in hand, and understanding the latter might be impossible without the former, says Zoltán Kövecses, professor of linguistics:

> *Emotion language is largely metaphorical in English and in all probability in other languages as well. [Metaphor is necessary] to capture the variety of diverse and intangible emotional experiences. Methodologically, then, this language is important in finding out about these experiences. The language, however, is not only a reflection of the experiences but it also creates them. Simply put, we say what we feel and we feel what we say.*[23]

As they pay more attention to the emotional drivers of consumer behavior, marketers begin to understand the importance of using deep metaphors in determining which emotions are relevant to their brands. That is, marketers learn which emotions influence how consumers evaluate their needs and the people, brands, and companies offering to help address those needs. What's more, once marketers understand the anatomy of these emotions, they can learn how to engage the emotions using metaphoric cues in product design, shopping environments, and other communications. While metaphors are central to identifying emotions, measures of metaphor properties are not to be confused with measures of emotions.

Managers must understand deep metaphors to avoid miscommunications. In fact, what marketers say is often not what consumers hear. Deep metaphors account for the difference.[24] Consider a food products firm that originally segmented its markets according to product features. Before its deep metaphor research, the company spoke to consumers narrowly, using only product-attribute language rather than the language of emotions that made those attributes important. According to a corporate insider, the company had been "addressing consumers in 'chemist speak,' while consumers were listening emotionally. The resulting conversation was not terribly productive." So the firm reoriented its segmentation according to a deep metaphor theme. In addition to addressing certain flavor qualities in its communications, the firm began to stress the cultural connections or associations triggered by those flavors, as the research also revealed that these connections were as important as taste in the purchase decision.

By probing deeper, a company can gain insights that it can convert into opportunities. For example, a major beverage company's standard market research had long determined that one of its primary brands rejuvenated and energized consumers. But the research had uncovered only *half* of its brand equity, the half that consumers could easily access and discuss. After conducting deep-level research similar to what we have described thus far, the company discovered that the brand also delivered inner peace and calm to consumers. With this new, deeper consumer insight, the company repositioned the brand to engage consumers in this new emotional terrain—and sales improved dramatically.

Finally, knowing which deep metaphors play in the unconscious minds of consumers can help managers think more deeply. A firm in the cell phone industry had been using product attribute preferences to segment markets. Declining revenues suggested that this approach was insufficient. Managers realized that they had failed to understand the emotional relevance of the benefits provided by particular product features. The firm embarked on an in-depth, multicountry study concerning parents' motivations for giving children cell phones. The resulting deeper insights produced a more useful segmentation strategy. Altogether, four key consumer segments were identified and subsequently validated by other techniques. All segments, it was found, shared the deep metaphor we call connection. However, the segments differed in how connection mattered. For instance, one group of consumers emphasized parent-child connections revolving around safety, evidenced in the group's disproportionate emphasis on security issues, as reflected in such statements as "The cell phone is like having a LoJack attached to the kids," "She has a sort of air bag with her, like in a car, in case she gets into trouble," and "It's like the EPIRB (emergency distress signaling device) on our boat." This new segmentation scheme has enabled the firm's product development and design teams and communications specialists to think more imaginatively, more meaningfully, and with greater resonance about consumer needs. The marketers are no longer thinking about consumers in shallow terms of product attributes, but in deeper emotional terms.

Seven Giants

In some twelve thousand in-depth interviews for more than a hundred clients in over thirty countries, seven deep metaphors have surfaced with the greatest frequency in every sector— finance, food, transportation, and so forth—and in every country, regardless of the research team. For example, our licensee in

Mexico came up with the same deep metaphors as those that our licensees in China and India uncovered for the same product. In short, these seven metaphors—balance, transformation, journey, container, connection, resource, and control—seem to have the most universality among consumers.

Though they are not characters like the storied Seven Dwarfs from *Snow White*, the metaphors are equally enduring across generations and cultures. Recall how the dwarfs capture qualities familiar to everyone: Dopey represents sweetness and silliness; Doc represents wisdom and intellect. Sneezy expresses our need to anticipate and manage certain physiological responses, and Sleepy expresses the tension between alternative states, which in his case are wakefulness and sleep. Meanwhile, Grumpy, Happy, and Bashful, like Dopey, express universal emotions and dispositions. The seven deep metaphors, or giants, explored in this book are even more personal. They are also the dominant characters in the land of Metaphoria.

People who otherwise differ in cultural background, age, gender, education, occupation, political values, consumer experiences, basic beliefs, religious preference, and almost anything else we can name share these seven giants. The metaphors are so robust that they extend across topics ranging from our choice of laundry detergent to our choice of president. For example, people in very different cultures or who differ in other ways tend to use the deep metaphor of balance to understand their job experiences, plan meals, and judge automobile designs. Of course, balance, like other deep metaphors, may be expressed differently in different cultures. People in China, Brazil, the United States, and Turkey use the same deep metaphors for oral care, cleaning clothes, and teaching nutrition to children, although the exact nature of their experience of these giants is not identical.

A study conducted for Procter & Gamble in France, the United States, and Japan about shopping experiences found that consumers in all three countries viewed shopping as a transformational journey, involving themes of work and play, among others. Concerning the work aspect of the shopping journey, a Japanese consumer noted feeling a "depressed, blue feeling so that I don't want to do anything. I don't ever want to see the products themselves much less go out and get them." A French consumer noted, "I am neither very happy nor very worried. It's just what you have to do; it's a path every mother with a family has to travel. I think, 'OK let's go and do the shopping and get it over with.'" A U.S. consumer commented, "I dread the trip to the supermarket because it is a means to an end. It is something we have to have, but not something I want to have. Because I buy the same thing every week, it is a very mundane and routine outing." These and other consumers in the study described other, more positive dimensions of the shopping journey, emphasizing a playful excursion and an exciting exploration. This example also illustrates that a deep metaphor may have multiple themes, often involving a bright and dark side.

The same person will use the same deep metaphor differently in different contexts. For instance, the experience of transformation when one is watching a Broadway play is not the same transformation one experiences in becoming a first-time parent or receiving a promotion at work.

These qualities of deep metaphors are identical to their siblings, emotions. For example, the fear of snakes is not the same as fear of public speaking or the fear of being caught in a tornado, and the sadness of losing a loved one is not the same sadness a player feels when losing a championship game. People in different cultures may also experience and express sadness with the same event differently.

Just as there is no one emotion that is inherently more important or typically precedes another, there is no hierarchy among the deep metaphors. Hence, the order in which we present them in this chapter and in the rest of the book is arbitrary. Where more than one deep metaphor matters in a given situation, as often happens, it is a classic circular issue. Which metaphor came first? Which matters more? The metaphors that are relevant depend on the situation. Importantly, managers can also influence a situation to make a desired metaphor prominent. For example, an advertisement showing a child sitting in a tire cues the container metaphor (Michelin), whereas a tire ad showing a fist griping the road cues the metaphor of control (Pirelli).

These seven giants—balance, transformation, journey, container, connection, resource, and control—account for about 70 percent of all the deep metaphors we have encountered in our consumer research. Since they have the most universality among consumers, they naturally have the most relevance for marketers, especially to fuel workable wondering. Again, more than one deep metaphor may be operating in a given situation, and the expression of one metaphor may contain telltale signs of the others.

Balance

Balance (imbalance) includes ideas of equilibrium, adjusting, maintaining or offsetting forces, and things as they should be. It has many flavors, including physical balance, moral balance, social balance, and aesthetic and psychological balance. In diet and eating, consumers reveal imbalance in expressions about being overweight or stuffed, while foods that complement each other reflect balance. Social imbalance appears in utterances about marrying above or below one's status, while employment balance turns up in equal opportunity policies, getting one's due, or earning grades. People express psychological imbalance when talking about being out-of-sorts, down, and feeling off, and psychological balance when they say they feel centered, feel inner peace, or are back on track.

Transformation

Transformation involves changing states or status. Physically, we can go from being "laid low by a cold" to being "up and about," and an antidepressant medication can change a depressed person's outlook on life. Emotionally, if we undergo a major life change, we talk about needing "attitude adjustments" or "turning over a new leaf." Mothers often think of their role as transformational; that is, to ensure that their children grow—or transform—physically and emotionally into healthy, functioning adults. But perhaps nothing connotes transformation better than nature's ultimate version: a humble caterpillar's changing into a beautiful butterfly. Hence, we see butterflies used in hospital designs and in advertisements promoting sleep aids. Transformations can be surprising or expected. Consumers may actively seek or avoid them. For example, children put on makeup to play adult roles whereas adults use makeup to retain a youthful appearance.

Journey

Consumers talk about many aspects of life as a journey. In fact, we often frame life itself as one big journey, including, for many, an afterlife. Sometimes we think of our lives as a brief journey, as in "life is short"; other times we view it as lengthy, as in "he still had so much life to live," when a journey ends prematurely. Confucius purportedly said, "A journey of a thousand miles begins with a single step." Consider Robert Frost's famous poem, *The Road Not Taken*, in which the speaker says, "Two roads diverged in a wood, and I took the one less traveled." Like Confucius, Frost conveys the unknown nature of many journeys. Other journeys have predictable outcomes, such as knowing that if you "stay on track" at work, you will earn a promotion. Journeys can be fast or slow—"time flies" but "are we there yet?"—or be "an uphill climb" or "all downhill from here."

Container

Containers perform two functions: keeping things in and keeping things out. They can protect us or trap us, can be opened and closed, and be positive or negative. They involve physical, psychological, and social states. We find ourselves in or out of physical shape or condition, in a good or bad mood, stuck in a rut, unable to kick a habit, or born into a social class and family. We prize our privacy, yet feel that others can read us like a book. We take time out or get back into an activity, we feel vulnerable or snug and secure, empty or fulfilled, wrapped up in a novel or left out on the street. We store up our money, energy, and goodwill. Memories are one of the most vital containers because they store our individual histories and identities.

Connection

Connection (disconnection) encompasses feelings of belonging or exclusion: being kept in or out of the loop, identifying with heroes, drawn to celebrities, or breaking up a relationship. We express psychological ownership when we say my brand, my team, my candidate, my kind of person, and MySpace. Feelings of distance and separation from others reflect disconnection, as when losing a friend, missing a pet, or losing a job. Similarly, we cannot shake a cold or get rid of certain people or recurring dreams. Themes of connection and disconnection factor prominently in consumers' thinking about marriage and divorce, having or adopting children, sending the kids to college, and giving and receiving gifts.

Resource

We need resources to survive. We would die without food and water or a nurturing adult in our infancy. Our family and friends are resources who support us in tough times and serve as what singer-songwriters Simon and Garfunkel called "a bridge over troubled water." In fact, all our giant deep metaphors—our mysterious tunes—populate the songs and other expressions of popular culture around the world. Products and services are also important resources: a woman refers to her cell phone as her "lifeline," and a man describes motor oil as his truck's "lifeblood." Companies also think of their product offerings as resources. For example, Dell may make MP3 players and other gadgets, but its "bread and butter" is the computer. We find resources in nature, manmade creations, or both: a natural athlete hones her skills and deems bottled spring water more healthful and enjoyable than high-calorie soft drinks. Knowledge and information are other vital resources. An intelligent person is a "fountain of knowledge"; gaining an education is the "key" to one's future.

Control

We human beings need to feel in control of our lives. Sometimes we succeed, sometimes we do not. When people "succumb" to a serious disease, they may feel "powerless." Or they may vow not to let "this thing ruin my life." When a lawyer rests a case, she may say the outcome is "out of our hands now," whereas during the case, she may have vowed to "fight to the finish." In our busy lives, we sometimes feel events "spiraling out of control." When life is calm, we cruise on "auto pilot." We describe ourselves or others as "out of control" or "uncontrollable" with respect to habits or addictions, blowing our stack, having a meltdown, throwing a tantrum, or acting as a tyrant. We may lose or regain bodily functions after entrusting ourselves to a surgeon, medication, or a physical therapist. We speak of span of control and decision rights within organizations and of leaders gaining or losing authority. We tame and train animals and feel at the mercy of nature. Social norms arise to control group interactions, and we imprison those who cannot follow those norms.

Other Deep Metaphors

The seven giants most permeate our lives. Indeed, few of our own research projects fail to uncover at least one giant metaphor as highly relevant, regardless of topic or cultural setting, and independent research teams in different organizations around the globe typically find one or more of these seven deep metaphors. Nevertheless, other deep metaphors such as movement or motion, force, nature, and system can be very relevant and have strategic importance, depending on the topic. We present a few of them briefly below and elsewhere in this book. As we have said, consumers may use more than one deep metaphor or viewing lens in a given situation. For example, the deep metaphors of journey, resource, force, and orientation surface in this slot machine player's description of the casino gambling experience: "It is like going on a rollercoaster (journey). You have exciting ups, then your stomach-churning downs (movement and orientation). You hope that luck (resource) will grab you and not let go (force). That is what I look forward to (orientation)."

MOVEMENT/MOTION. This deep metaphor has much in common with journey and is often an element of a journey. Humans need to feel as if they are moving forward, either with the task at hand, their day, or more significantly, through life. We do not want to feel stagnant or "stuck." Interactions with others are the same way. In some cases, relationships move fast, we instantly click with someone; our relationship is on track, moving along. We can also, however, feel that a relationship has hit a "dead end" or is no longer progressing. We avoid situations that lack movement; we try to "keep things going." A lot of motion can remind people of energy and vitality, and we prefer to be a "mover and shaker," not a slacker.

FORCE. Force manifests itself as power, a powerful presence, or a source of energy. Consumers also describe force as a physical impact: getting slammed or hit. Companies use this metaphor in advertisements to demonstrate strong or lasting flavor, to "shock" you or "set your mouth on fire." Consumers might describe frustration with a company as "banging one's head against a wall" trying to get through to someone. Positively, one might combine force and movement to describe a transaction that happened in a "flash." People can also feel as if life is a force. In a study of generalized anxiety disorder, for example, participants describe anxiety as a powerful force pushing down on them, one that would attack them at any given moment without notice. In fact, much like movement/motion is a "sibling" metaphor to journey, force is a sibling to control.

NATURE. Depending on the product, consumer references to the outdoors and nature can be very important. Nature represents what does not come from man. Natural products are uncontaminated and pristine. For example, a denture cream product may sell more effectively if consumers consider it natural, as opposed to industrial or abrasive. Nature symbolizes growth or evolution. But the natural can also be opposed to the civilized life. A motorcycle study, for example, demonstrated that consumers saw themselves as at one with nature while they were riding "wild and untamed."

SYSTEM. This deep metaphor arises when consumers need order or structure. For example, in reference to our biological system, we often refer to athletes as "well-oiled machines" or the elderly as "breaking down." When a market crashes or a market leader falls, there is often a "domino effect," and when we fail to finalize a deal or to communicate our grand vision, we claim that there were just "too many moving parts." We establish intricate rituals and procedures in our lives, and when we do not follow them, we feel "disjointed." When someone is of unsound mind, we may refer to them as "having a screw loose."

Some Cautions About Deep Metaphors

We judge a particular deep metaphor to be present when many
people in a study express it multiple times in their surface metaphors. The mere occurrence of a deep metaphor expression does
not alone suggest its importance. Also, just because an object, a
place, an event, or a service literally involves a deep metaphor, it
does not mean that this metaphor is the primary viewing lens.
For example, in a project on packaging conducted for a leading
over-the-counter medication, control and resource rather than
container were the primary deep metaphors. In studies for a
cruise line and an airline, we anticipated references to journey,
but found that transformation and container, respectively, were
more important to the travelers' assessment of their experiences.

Again, different deep metaphors may apply to different
brands in the same category. Budweiser owns the connection
metaphor, whereas Coors owns nature and movement. We find
similar contrasts among sporting apparel brands, motorcycles,
automobiles, and so on. Often, too, different brands will involve different themes of the same deep metaphor.

Sometimes, marketers need to change the deep metaphors
consumers use, and sometimes, marketers need only to leverage
the metaphors. Using the right deep metaphor in the wrong
way can lead consumers to hear something very different from
what was intended. For example, one bank experiencing growth
problems chose community resource as the deep metaphor for
repositioning itself among consumer and business accounts.
How the bank communicated this positioning in printed materials and how bank employees behaved gave consumers the impression that the community was a resource *for the bank*, rather
than the bank's being a resource for the community. The bank

quickly detected and corrected this miscommunication before the wrong frame could firmly establish itself among consumers.

Summary

Managers should worry about depth deficits, that is, the lack of careful reflection and bold thinking about rich consumer information. Shallow thinking has many causes, including having out-of-date knowledge about how the mind works, discouraging work environments, and the simple fear of thinking differently. There is yet another cause of depth deficits: an overemphasis on differences among consumers—an overemphasis that blinds managers to the more important underlying dimensions about which consumers may vary.

Managers must do the following:

- Obtain deep insights from consumers to think deeply in productive ways. This involves having workable knowledge and engaging in workable wondering

- Understand the common dimensions that give rise to apparent differences in the marketplace

- Identify and leverage the basic viewing lenses—the deep metaphors—that seemingly different people have in common

Attending to deep metaphors can help managers uncover consumers' hidden thoughts and feelings, overcome the say-mean gap, uncover brand- and category-relevant emotions, and think more deeply when developing and implementing marketing strategy.

2

Foundations
of Deep Metaphors

*How Managers Benefit
from Discovering Consumer Similarities*

The human ability to observe differences in ourselves and our environment originates in a highly developed, innate capacity for making contrasts. At a very basic level, this capacity allows us to survive.[1] We can distinguish between a moving car and a stationary one when crossing a busy street. We can tell whether the smell or the composition of the milk in the carton has changed overnight. We can compare the consequences of alternative actions, thus enabling ourselves to learn how to walk, speak a language, form social relationships, take responsibility for our actions, or design better products, services, and communications for consumers and employees.

Our ability to perceive differences is so well developed that we even find differences where none exist. For instance, when comparing clearly labeled wines or beers or soft drinks, people will detect taste differences, whereas in unlabeled taste tests of the same products, tasters often detect no differences. People will insist that one brand of medication acts more quickly and effectively than another brand, even when the medicines are identical in their chemical composition. The mere belief that something is different (when it is not) can actually induce measurable albeit temporary changes in our experiences, as patients sometimes encounter when taking placebos. Not surprisingly, differences capture our attention.

We detect differences so automatically that marketers can easily overlook a significant fact: differences stem from similarities. Differences surround a finite number of commonalities. In fact, *we cannot make comparisons—the essence of noting differences—without referring to an underlying common dimension*. We cannot say one salesperson is aggressive and another is passive without reference to the underlying dimension of forwardness. Consumers describe one service provider as prompt and another as always late—a comparison whose gauge is a basic notion of responsiveness. They use an underlying dimension of fairness when viewing one price as a rip-off and another, lower price for the same product as a bargain. Using underlying dimensions such as responsiveness and fairness as viewing lenses helps us avoid chaos and organize our experiences.

Our point here is simple but important: in marketers' efforts to identify and communicate some distinct benefit or unique selling proposition, they often give too much weight to differences and pay too little attention to the underlying deep metaphors or viewing lenses consumers use to detect and interpret those differences. This imbalance should surprise no one, since noticing differences occupies our conscious minds while the operation of underlying common or shared dimensions occurs primarily in our unconscious minds. Even here we cannot avoid using the underlying dimension of awareness to distinguish between conscious and unconscious thinking.

You already recognize such acknowledged commonalities as primary emotions, core needs, and basic values. In the remainder of this chapter, we explore the cornerstones of deep metaphors, a neglected commonality that shapes what we think, hear, say, and do.

Pattern Recognition

Our penchant for detecting differences would soon produce chaos, were it not for the countervailing ability to notice patterns. Nobel Prize winner Gerald Edelman points out, "There are two main modes of thought—pattern recognition and logic [and] the primary mode, giving enormous range in confronting novelty, is pattern recognition."[2] Our ability to see meaningful patterns rather than be overwhelmed by differences enables us to determine where to find food, what is poisonous and what is edible, who are friends and who are enemies, and which financial investments to make and which to forgo. For instance, simply by observing facial patterns, we can identify with surprising ease and accuracy the emotions of others, even complete strangers with ethnically different facial features and expressions.[3]

In detecting patterns, we locate essences or bundles of reference points. This capacity enables us to distinguish realism from abstract art, classical music from jazz, and wine from beer.

The ability to recognize patterns gives meaning to our lives. Master violinist Yehudi Menuhin expresses this nicely: "Music creates order out of chaos, for rhythm imposes unanimity upon the divergent, melody imposes continuity upon the disjointed, and harmony imposes compatibility upon the incongruous."[4] Life would be chaotic, to say the least, if we only experienced differences or if our proclivity for noticing differences overpowered that for noticing similarities.

Pattern recognition involves conscious and unconscious thought. However, we tend to engage our conscious minds when noticing differences, thus getting an impression that differences are pervasive. On the other hand, our unconscious minds will more likely be engaged when we employ unifying dimensions to make conscious distinctions. We do not think explicitly about forwardness when noticing that one salesperson is more passive than another. We do not think explicitly about underlying style when first noticing an impressionist painting that attracts us versus one that repels us. But without an underlying basic dimension, we cannot meaningfully notice much at all.

Pattern recognition is central to another process, categorization, which helps us understand deep metaphors. We look at categorization next.

Categorization: The Many Uses of a Shark

Deep metaphors are categories of viewing lenses. For example, people may think about financial planning as "a rocky road," "an uphill battle," "like wandering aimlessly," "an exciting, challenging adventure," "smooth sailing," and so on. These specific lenses are instances of a larger category, namely, journey. Since deep metaphors are basic categories of patterned thinking and decision making, managers should understand how categorization works in the minds of consumers.

Categorization is the process of identifying specific features of an object, a place, or an event as an instance of a more general example of that object, place, or event. Thus, there are many kinds of animals but only one called cat. There are many kinds of cats but only one called calico. Through direct and mediated experience, we learn that cats differ from dogs. No matter how many kinds of dogs we encounter, they are unmistakably dogs and not cats, snakes, or birds. Of course, we learn or are taught broader categories and thus know that both cats and dogs are mammals rather than reptiles, insects, or plants.

Consumers develop categories for just about everything. Whether it is a pickup game in the park or the final match of the World Cup, football is football, and not cricket or hockey. We learn that certain clouds portend thunderstorms and others herald fair weather, one part of the city is congested in the morning and another is not, and one manager's face is friendly but another's is intimidating. Whether we are correct or mistaken in how we categorize patterns of clouds, traffic, or managerial disposition, we do it automatically. Our categories typically come to our conscious attention only when we cannot automatically determine which category to use or if we have clearly erred in our choice.

Categories are devices for making sense of the world, and like all devices, they are not foolproof. When we categorize (or label) a person, we impose on that person our beliefs about the category—and we may not simply be categorizing the person as African American, Anglo, or Hispanic, poor or rich, blue-collar or white-collar, gay or straight; we may be pigeonholing or stereo-typing someone, making oversimplified or exaggerated and frequently offensive generalizations about him or her. Consider the series of popular advertisements for the Government Employees Insurance Company (GEICO) featuring Neanderthal-like cavemen who behave as any affluent, educated, and cultured consumer would. The ads play on the cavemen's negative reaction to the stereotypical caveman captured in the mock tagline, "GEICO: so easy a caveman could do it."

We may place the same person, place, event, or object in more than one category. Consumers sometimes categorize snack foods as "unhealthy excesses" and other times as "special treats." Which category people choose reveals something about them in that particular moment, and their beliefs about categories overall reveal much about them and about their knowledge, emotions, experience, biases, tastes, and upbringing. For example, while developing an electric-powered vehicle, one automobile manufacturer learned that some consumers categorize these vehicles as simply cars with oversized batteries, while other consumers saw the vehicles as supercomputers. These different categorizations corresponded to differences in consumer sensitivity to environmental concerns: the oversized-battery group was less concerned about the environment than the supercomputer group was.

Images from one category help us think about objects, events, or experiences belonging to other categories.[5] Since a consensus usually exists about the nature of categories, we often use them automatically to convey information about quite unrelated items. Without this ability, we could not express and explain our thoughts and actions very well. For example, how often do you refer to fish in the course of a day? Fish live in water, which they constantly gulp, and so a person who abuses alcohol "drinks like a fish." An extremely quiet person is "mute as a fish." When fish hit dry land, they flop about and die, and so we feel "like a fish out of water" when experiencing social awkwardness. We feel as if we are "swimming upstream" when struggling toward a difficult but important goal. We "smell something fishy" when we suspect foul play. The behavior of particular fish helps us convey the unsavory qualities of certain people such as loan sharks and card sharks. The names for many products and services leverage thoughts about one category to enhance thoughts about brands. For example, a mustang conveys ideas about a particular Ford car. Chevy trucks are "like a rock." "Nothing runs like a Deere" denotes a brand of farm equipment. Wheaties cereal is "the breakfast of champions," and Budweiser is "the King of Beers" to denote their positions in the hierarchy of brands. Life insurance companies use ideas associated with various symbols such as umbrellas (Travelers), rocks (Prudential Insurance Company), and hands (Allstate) to convey qualities of protection, sturdiness, and support.

Archetypes: Categories of Greatness

Most people know of archetypes such as the wise elder or the great mother as original models or prototypes after which or after whom other things or people are patterned. These archetypes are generic or idealized representations of someone or something usually likened to a certain personality type or characteristic. Archetypes pervade literature. In fact, the Seven Dwarfs introduced earlier are personality archetypes: Grumpy, Happy, and so on. The psychologist Carl G. Jung argued that archetypes are patterns, symbols, and images that represent basic qualities of mind inherent in and shared by every person, regardless of culture. Hence, archetypes are universal and operate in what Jung called our "collective unconscious."

His views have greatly influenced psychoanalysis, literary analysis, film studies, and marketing research and practice. People have developed his ideas into numerous so-called human archetypes such as hero, outlaw, magician, innocent, shape-shifter, explorer, creator, caregiver, sage, jester, and ruler. Each archetype has its own defining characteristics and variations that marketers have leveraged in building their brands. For example, Harley-Davidson, associated with breaking rules, symbolizes the outlaw. The Marlboro Man, associated with the Western frontier, stands for the adventurer. The Oprah Book Club, which helps people understand their world, calls up the sage.[6]

For marketers, archetypes can help describe central tendencies in consumers' behavior or the role that brands and companies play for consumers. British retailer Marks and Spencer observed what we call orphanlike behavior in men who wandered aimlessly around the store, looking confused and out of place. Apparently unsure of whom to ask for help, these men demonstrated unfamiliarity with their female partners' clothing size and color preferences and fled the store as if escaping from a hostile environment. Marks and Spencer reported that only one-third of the men studied knew the sizes and color preferences of the female partners for whom they were shopping. Not surprisingly, only one-third of the women surveyed were satisfied with the gifts that these men purchased. Consequently, the retailer introduced an easily identifiable and quite friendly-looking salesperson called "Stocking Fella," a combination of the sage, savior, and Santa Claus archetypes, to help these "orphan" men during shopping.[7]

The use of human archetypes to describe our experiences with brands, companies, or other aspects of consumption reflects our tendency to anthropomorphize—to ascribe human form and personalities to nonhuman entities and events. As a result, marketers often design research to discover archetypes by specifically asking consumers what kind of person or what kind of animal best describes a brand or store. This approach introduces a bias, however. Human and animal qualities are not the only lens, nor even the primary lens, that people use to judge the products and services they consume or the firms that provide them. That a consumer will answer such questions does not mean that the answers reflect how he or she actively think about the brand or company. So, while human and other archetypes can reveal important consumer thoughts, marketers must elicit them naturally; that is, the archetypes must emerge automatically and spontaneously so that the consumer rather than the researcher is introducing them into the discussion.

Like the archetypes they sometimes contain, deep metaphors are abstractions; they categorize patterns of thought that create our viewing lenses. These metaphors are more comprehensive than personality types, although certain archetypical personalities might be encompassed by deep metaphors. Deep metaphors, then, are broader and more fundamental to cognitive processes than the personality archetypes derived from Jung's original thinking. Of course, personality archetypes can lead to insights relevant to marketing research and communications, but they cover only a limited part of how consumers think.

Recognizing and categorizing patterns are processes that ultimately stem from the partnership between social settings and our minds. See the discussion of this complex activity in "The Mind Is What the Brain Does."

The Mind Is What the Brain Does

Leading cognitive neuroscientists believe that *the mind is what the brain does*.[a] That is, all our thoughts and feelings, conscious or unconscious, are qualities of *mind* that occur because of firings among a particular set of neurons in our *brain*. For this reason, mind and brain are basically indistinguishable. Firings among neurons produce a thought that is likely to activate other neurons, whose multiple firings yield other thoughts. These thoughts are concepts. A set of concepts that are activated together are variously called mental models, maps, frames, and image schema. We possess models or schema about nearly every situation in life, ranging from what constitutes an appropriate brand of nail polish to finding a mate.

Deep metaphors are outcomes of these complex neural activities. Both right and left brain hemispheres—and multiple sites within each hemisphere—are involved in processing metaphors.[b] The activation of a deep metaphor involves a neural signature, a network of neural activations. Nobelist Gerald Edelman notes that thought can take place without language: "In its earliest form, thought is dependent on metaphorical modes."[c] Steven Pinker affirms this as well: "I think that metaphor really is a key to explaining thought and language."[d] For example, when a brand succeeds in establishing a basic association (literally, a neural pathway) in consumers' minds, subsequent activations of this association increase the strength of the pathway so that an entire neural network eventually forms to reinforce it. The beer brewer Anheuser-Busch has repeatedly used the idea of connection as its deep metaphor in advertising its Budweiser brand over time, so that Budweiser owns that association. Consumers' minds implicitly associate Budweiser and social connection. The association hinders other brands from making the same association, and when one of Anheuser-Busch's competitors uses social connection, consumers will think of Budweiser as well.

When neurons from different brain regions fire together, they form connections that create ideas. Consequently, no matter how well we understand the neurological structure and functioning of the brain (and there is still much to learn) we cannot identify a single place in the brain that contains the essence of a specific idea, much less a deep metaphor. There is no single identifiable "spot in the brain," as Jerome Kagan puts it, where Einstein developed the theory of relativity, where Boston's baseball fans developed their commitment to the Red Sox, or where the popular GEICO gecko or the Aflac duck influences consumers in the United States and Japan. The scattered nature of the origin of particular thoughts and feelings in the brain resembles the contagion of a crowd, found not in a specific person, but in the collective.[e]

The same cerebral sites may be activated for very different reasons and hence represent different thoughts. That is partly why a particular deep metaphor may, with different twists, operate in different situations. This activation parallels that of emotions. For instance, an advertisement intended to arouse fear could activate the amygdala, a part of the brain involved in emotions. But both positive and negative stimuli can cause surprise without involving fear. Fear and surprise—such as an *ooh-aah* response to the design of the ad—produce similar activations in the amygdala.

Even precise measures of active brain sites, while helpful, do not tell us the *content of a thought*, such as whether a person is feeling guilt or shame, fear or surprise, or something else. Nor do precise measurements tell us which of several forms of a deep metaphor such as balance may be operating. Marketers must conduct research that reveals whether consumers are experiencing guilt, shame, embarrassment, or some other feeling or whether social or moral imbalance is operating. Furthermore, the meaning of guilt will vary considerably, depending on its context. Guilt elicited by a life insurance advertisement will differ from guilt elicited by an advertisement for diet pills or automobile tires.

a. *This necessarily oversimplified description is used commonly by such scientists as Stephen M. Kosslyn, Steven Pinker, Daniel Siegel, Antonio Damasio, Edmund Rolls, and others whose works are cited throughout this book.*

b. See, for example, Alexander M. Rapp et al., "Neural Correlates of Metaphor Processing," *Cognitive Brain Research* 20 (2004), 395–402.

c. Gerald M. Edelman, *Second Nature: Brain Science and Human Knowledge* (New Haven, CT: Yale University Press, 2006), 153.

d. Steven Pinker, *The Stuff of Thought: Language as a Window Into Human Nature* (New York: Viking, 2007), 276.

e. Jerome Kagan, *An Argument for Mind* (New Haven, CT: Yale University Press, 2006), 223.

Embodied Cognition

Our senses and motor systems provide categories that contribute greatly to how we perceive, understand, and express abstract thoughts and feelings. This categorization is referred to as *embodied cognition*.[8] Embodied cognition is reflected in the metaphors we use in daily language. In this book, for example, we hope you "see" what we mean and "get the point." We want the idea to "sound" right, not to "stink." We will explain where we are "going" or "coming from" with this thought, and trust you are "up to" understanding. Executives solve messy problems by "charging ahead" or "taking one step at a time." When a problem goes away, we feel a "weight lifted from our shoulders" and no longer "feel down." As Edelman points out, "we must pay attention to the observation that the brain is embodied and therefore the brain and the body interact critically with each other. Moreover, both are embedded in the real world, which obviously has an enormous influence on these dynamics."[9]

Our senses and motor systems are essential devices for developing and expressing thoughts. They enable us to

- Monitor and understand the world around and within us

- Describe our experiences to others

- Take appropriate actions

Vision is a frequent source of embodied cognition. This is not surprising, given that more than 60 percent of stimuli reaching the brain do so via the visual system. We describe a joke as off-color; we refer to certain verbal expressions as colorful or graphic; someone with a strong sense of purpose is a visionary; attractive or unusual things are eye-catching; a disorganized person is unfocused; and people who cannot plan or look ahead are myopic while those who can are farsighted. Organizations have vision statements, maintain a customer focus, keep an eye on their competition, look ahead, and fail to use their peripheral vision.[10]

Similarly, we use all our senses to convey thoughts not directly tied to those senses. We are touched by a story, thick- (or thin-) skinned when receiving criticism, have warm or cold hearts, deserve a tongue lashing, are asked to bite our tongue when restraint is needed, are accused of listening but not hearing, allow things to go in one ear and out the other, have bittersweet experiences, and see others as stepping on our toes.

Our sense of physical orientation is another major source of metaphor. We want to get ahead, not fall behind, keep up with the pack, not fall down on the job, rise to the occasion, move up the corporate ladder, grow our savings, not throw in the towel, avoid becoming washed up, grasp difficult concepts, not get stepped on, avoid knee-jerk reactions, and so on. One colleague, Jack Carew, has shared over one hundred ways we metaphorically use the simple word *up*.[11] Here are just a few examples: "What's up? The stock market is up. He is on the up-and-up. I feel up. She is moving up in the company." In general, there are many more positive connotations with the word *up* than with the word *down*.

By using our sensory and motor systems, having an awareness of our bodies generally, and maintaining a sense of orientation, we have developed basic frames for a myriad of experiences, with our body as a primary "yardstick." The concept of balance, for example, forms very early in life. The idea of container, that is, something—be it our mind, stomach, home, schedule—that holds certain things and excludes others, also originates in reference to our body. In fact, all deep metaphors frequently use our sense of body as a key mode of expression. Thus, our anatomy and physiology—figuratively and literally—are key originators of deep metaphors.

Product design specialists find metaphors reflecting embodied cognition particularly helpful. For instance, the redesign of an all-terrain vehicle is being guided by such expressions as "It makes me feel like a giant fist," "It makes me soar emotionally," "As soon as I get on, I feel up," and "I get this towering sensation." These expressions help shape the design guidelines or principles: various design and feature options are evaluated for their resonance with the deeper ideas behind these expressions. Similarly, a leading consumer goods firm identified several new-product opportunities for men's body care products by understanding various sensory and motor system metaphors consumers used when discussing health care, their appearance, and social acceptance.

Social Connections Affect Neural Connections

Brain activity shapes, and is shaped by, what other brains do. In other words, other people greatly influence the wiring of any one person's brain. Daniel J. Siegel underscores these influences on brain formation:

> *Relationship experiences have a dominant influence on the brain because the circuits responsible for social perception are the same as or tightly linked to those that integrate the important functions controlling the creation of meaning, the regulation of bodily states, the modulation of emotion, the organization of memory, and the capacity for interpersonal communication. Interpersonal experience thus plays a special organizing role in determining the development of brain structure early in life and the ongoing emergence of brain function throughout the lifespan.[12]*

Nature endows us with many possible neural connections to accommodate the very different "settings" required or favored by our circumstances at birth and throughout life. The brain pares away connections used infrequently and potential connections never used (thus, the expression "Use it or lose it").[13] This paring begins with an infant's early bonding experiences with an adult. Even some language conditioning occurs prenatally. As we interact with our cultural and physical environments, we stabilize some neural connections and eliminate the surplus.[14] To be sure, basic predispositions such as temperament exist at birth and can have important, enduring effects.[15] But social and physical environments affect the manifestation of people's predispositions.[16] Edelman expands this observation: "The epigenetic and historical changes in the formation of brain maps are strongly affected by the signals from the body and environment. This is true during fetal development as well as in development after birth."[17]

Many environments influence us concurrently and over time: parents, school, peer groups, religious community, geography, and historical events, to name some of the most common. However, even very different groups must solve similar problems, and they often do so in remarkably similar ways.[18] Consequently, basic similarities arise in the mind or brain configurations of very different people who are addressing similar situations. That is why, when probing deeply into the minds of seemingly different consumers, we find the same basic deep metaphors used for the same issues. Moreover, we can explore the minds of only a few people to identify the deep metaphors shared by far more people.[19] Finally, because the brain follows parsimonious yet robust organizing principles, a relatively small number of deep metaphors apply to many diverse circumstances, as we will see.

Summary

Humans have a natural tendency to notice differences. However, we can observe meaningful differences only by using a common denominator—the dimension about or around which people differ. Whether we are noting differences or similarities, we are relying on a fundamental ability, the ability to detect patterns. By detecting patterns, we can place objects, persons, and events in particular categories. A category is a collection of like items that share a common essence. Categories are vital to our making sense of the world around us. Regardless of nationality or ethnicity, people generally agree about what does and does not belong in a particular category. This consensus enables us to use the characteristics found in one category of objects, events, or persons to convey ideas about people or things found in another category. For instance, consumers use the qualities of fish and, particularly, sharks to describe certain people or their behaviors. Anyone who has ever fished understands what a colleague means by "you are opening a can of worms with that grievance." Thus, pattern recognition and categorization are basic thinking processes and important foundations for deep metaphors. We noted that our bodies offer special subcategories that form an integral part of our metaphor usage. Archetypes are another categorization that provides a useful source of metaphors.

Deep metaphors are matters of mind, of course. And the mind is what the brain does. What the brain does is determined in a significant way by the external world. This partnership between neural connections and social connections provides the primary landscape for deep metaphors and assures their universality—different consumers can experience the same deep metaphors differently in different circumstances anywhere in the world. Managers can leverage the universality of deep metaphors in the development and implementation of marketing strategy.

3

Balance

How Justice, Equilibrium, and the Interplay
of Elements Affect Consumer Thinking

Balance describes a state of physical, psychological, or social equilibrium. As we near that state, we experience a
sense of balance; as we deviate we experience feelings of imbalance. Balance is one of the earliest manifestations of embodied
cognition. Often, multiple dimensions or elements are involved
as we look through this lens. Let's consider an example.

Before beginning the production and marketing of a premium vodka, a new distillery wanted to understand consumers'
thoughts and feelings about premium, or "top-shelf," brands
of vodka and why people drink it. This new spirits firm also
wanted to understand consumer responses to alternative concepts for a premium brand and alternative brand names. This
consumer feedback would help the firm position the new brand
in a highly competitive market.

In a series of studies, the deep metaphor of *balance* arose time and again. In particular, consumers discussed the balance between natural elements, represented by the freshness and general quality of ingredients, and nurture, represented by a handcrafted distilling process. One consumer noted, "The right ingredients in the wrong hands or the wrong ingredients in the right hands produce the same result: alcohol without any class. You know from the very first taste that the natural and human elements are off. They should be aligned." Another consumer expressed this theme in his description of a digital image (figure I-2 in color insert). Note how this consumer comments on a balance between natural and human contributions in the making of vodka as well as a balance between hard work and appropriate rewards.

The firm is using these insights to name their new brand "Upright." In testing research, they found that "Upright" captured the sense of authenticity in a premium vodka made with high-quality ingredients by high-quality distilling craftsmen. A brand named "Upright" suggests the kind of taste and general consumption experience that hardworking people feel they had earned—a just or fair reward for putting forth their best efforts in other areas of their lives.

The Origins of Balance As a Deep Metaphor

Balance has both biological and social foundations.[1] We call young children toddlers because, when first learning to walk, they easily toddle, fall, stumble, or otherwise lose their balance. One of our earliest lessons, then, is to maintain physical balance.[2] Similarly, our visual system engages in complicated optical dynamics for us to recognize shapes, movements, and colors in order to help us avoid becoming disoriented. We feel tense when looking at a design that violates certain visual principles involving balance. Our experiences of taste and indeed all our senses provide yet other experiences relating to balance. Many physiological states, when violated, create a sense of physical imbalance or discomfort: fever, vertigo, numbness, depression, dehydration, and so on. Disease refers to a physical state of being "not at ease."

Social scientists are discovering that humans have an inborn capacity, or a "grammar," for social fairness, morality, and justice. In other words, balance is a deeply rooted and basic human orientation to the world.[3] Everyday consumer language is rife with evocative surface metaphor expressions of balance. Consumers talk about "getting what you pay for," "being ripped off," and "it's not worth the expense." Employees talk about "a fair deal," "straightening out a mess," "getting what they deserve," and "walking a fine line." Similarly, managers encourage us to "use resources in moderation," "be fair," and "get both sides of a story."

A two-country study on privacy illustrates the interplay of the psychological and social dimensions of balance.[4] Consumers in both the United States and Japan felt that giving personal information to companies was fair as long as companies used it to the consumer's benefit, such as alerting people to sales on brands they frequently purchased. On the other hand, whenever they suspected their personal information had been sold to other vendors, many consumers felt morally indignant. One consumer said, "I just wish I could do the same to them, send their private information out to the rest of the world. Then, I'd feel a little better. I'd like to get even, but I can't. It is really frustrating."

Consumers want a company to "play by the same rules" and face the same consequences if it does not. When they perceive the scale has tipped to favor the company, consumers resent the injustice.

Balance Is Dynamic, Not a Fixed State

Balance is a fluid interplay between various dimensions rather than a fixed state. A cosmetics firm wanted to understand what the phrase *life spirit* meant for consumers. When researchers asked consumers in several countries to collect pictures of experiences that expressed this concept, the consumers chose images to represent contrasting states. For most people, the phrase meant achieving balance between calm and exciting activities, between private and public events, as well as between simple and complex goods and services.

In another study, researchers asked consumers to depict experiences of the "simple pleasures" of life. The respondents revealed a complex interplay between various types of experiences, each type playing a role in how the consumer achieved an overall sense of balanced well-being. When consumers felt "centered," they meant that they achieved a balanced mix of these experiences giving them a sense of being "just right." That point of "just rightness" varied from individual to individual. A combination of safe but exciting social pleasures—including interactions with pets and close friends or family members—mattered to all consumers. Feeling safe and yet free to be oneself enabled bold and expressive action, such as dancing, wearing bright colors or unusual clothing, traveling alone, learning new skills, and buying something very expensive.

Four Kinds of Balance

We express deep metaphors in many ways. This next section explores four broad but not exhaustive possibilities for how we express balance.

Physical Balance

Physical balance is a viewing lens central to the health and well-ness industry, among others. Whether citing guidelines about proper diet and exercise or the benefits of medication, supplements, treatment programs, and other practices, this huge industry assumes that our minds and bodies are naturally balanced and that deviations are unhealthy, bad, or dangerous.[5]

Balance is relevant for products referred to as nutri-cosmetics, beauty products that consumers can drink, apply directly to the skin, or even take as a pill. When caring for their skin, consumers seek beauty products that strike a balance between gentleness and effectiveness: "I need to feel it working but not as if I were giving my hands an acid bath, like some of the stuff I use at work feels," said one of our study participants. Clean, smooth skin also provides emotional balance by making people more relaxed and less worried about hygiene.

One consumer, when asked to create a digital image of metaphors for his hands, described his digital image as a depiction of an unbalanced state. This is not unusual—people often first explain what something is not (imbalance) before explaining what it is (balance): "Being a dentist and not doing manual labor like my father, a farmer, I associate the little white rabbit with the softness of my hands. The tractor represents my father's hands, very callused and scratched, and his fingernails are dirty." He sees his father as so focused on manual labor that his father cannot take care of his hands. By contrast, the dentist's hands are pure and unsullied. As the consumer continued to talk, he revealed an internal conflict between how he feels about his appearance to his patients and how he feels about his masculinity and hobbies that sully that image. For

him, wearing gloves is a compromise, balancing these conflicting needs.

In a study exploring the role of health ranch visits in their
lives, consumers described their body as a machine, broken
down by the stresses and obligations of daily life, and how
health ranches restored their body's balance. One person used a
picture of a car engine in serious disrepair: "This car with someone looking under the hood has steam coming from different
places and dripping oil. That is how I view going to the ranch—
like getting a body tune-up." The physical imbalances of the
body linked closely to emotional imbalances. Consumers often
mentioned needing repair and their worries about heart attacks
and other stress-related illnesses. Many consumers felt they were
expending too much energy caring for friends, family, and coworkers and not tending enough to their own needs. As a conse-
quence, they felt the need to "break free from the daily grind"
and to set aside restorative time. A visit to a health ranch
restored physical and emotional balance. Some consumers compared their bodies after this experience to a blooming flower—
clean, pure, and beautiful; light, yet full of life.

Emotional Balance

Emotional balance refers to appropriateness in our attitudes,
beliefs, knowledge, and general cognitive functioning.[6] A balanced person is viewed as "even-tempered," "at peace," "fair-
minded," "in the zone," "having a zest for life," "cool as a
cucumber," and "having his or her act together." We call imbalanced people "too emotional," "too put out," or "off their
rocker," or we say they have "lost their mind," or are "suffering
information overload."

Emotional balance often underlies consumers' thoughts and feelings about desserts. Consumers may seek the experience of having a calm, fun, free feeling by eating a healthy dessert while also expressing strong emotions about the consequences of eating the wrong dessert. For many consumers, there is a fuzzy line concerning the quantity of sweets that can be considered "nice" as opposed to "naughty." One participant captured this sentiment when describing her digital image, which contained a champagne bottle: "There is a fine balance between being physically and mentally healthy. The champagne bottle is floating in water with a pair of 'naughty girl' pants hanging from it. They symbolize the naughty-but-nice aspect of eating sweets. Nice to eat, but naughty if you eat too many."

Emotional balance plays a role in how we view many products. For example, Harley-Davidson owners describe their riding experience as a source of emotional balance in their daily lives. The pleasure and relaxation of riding offsets the monotony of work and the stresses of responsibility. Riders believe they gain emotional balance by becoming more in touch with their inner selves, feeling inner calm, confidence, and self-esteem. Harley-Davidson has used this insight to communicate that buying a Harley is much more than a motorcycle purchase—it is a form of therapy.

When General Motors asked consumers to describe car designs they found appealing, many drivers described a vehicle whose appearance is simultaneously emotionally soothing and exciting. A balance of both qualities provides the "just right" vehicle. Consumers also described the need to balance the appearance of the exterior of a vehicle with the way they experience the interior. Whether thinking of a luxury vehicle or low-end car, consumers want the interior and exteriors to be compatible; they feel uncomfortable with a luxurious exterior and a skimpy interior, and vice versa. Automobiles that coordinate the interior and exterior appropriately are much more likely to have consumers say, "I don't know what it is, but this car just feels right to me."

The Heinz Endowments for the Arts found that the arts effectively restore and maintain equilibrium in people's lives by increasing self-esteem, creating mental energy, allowing discovery, and imparting feelings of peace and relaxation. Self-esteem contributes to balance by engendering pride, confidence, and security. Energy contributes by providing emotional and physical stimulation, more endurance, and feelings of being refreshed and renewed. Discovery contributes to balance by providing something new and unexpected, offering a new perspective, delivering a welcome change or departure from the familiar. Being at peace contributes to balance by providing serenity, satisfaction, and freedom from anxiety or stress. The Heinz Endowments staff concluded that arts marketers must use all these ideas, in combination, to help consumers feel that the arts promote balance in their lives.

Emotional and physical balances often work in tandem. For example, a Japanese consumer products conglomerate wanted to bring its vegetable juices to the United States. The juices were created using a unique process called *lactic fermentation*. This proprietary process allowed the juices to be processed without the high heat associated with conventional canning and pasteurization—heat that destroys some of the vegetables' flavor and nutritional content. To help formulate the core idea of the product line and express the competitive position of the brand, the company needed to understand better how consumers conceptualized organic foods. According to our research, people believe that by eating improperly, they become "polluted or imbalanced." One participant put it, "Your stress level goes up when you're not emotionally balanced. When you're fatigued, your mind is not as clear—you get even more stressed. It's all just related to a balanced diet. If you had a balanced diet, you could deal with stressful situations better."

Basically, consumers say that when the wrong things enter the body, people become physically and emotionally out of balance and have trouble getting through their day. Without proper nutrition, one cannot function, and daily life is "thrown out of whack." But when talking about the role of organic vegetables in their lives, one consumer's words spoke for many: "The biggest part of the whole mindfulness and purification movement is to eat organic food because so many other foods have toxins or hormones that harm your body. The whole Buddhist principle is to put nothing but good food in your body to cleanse it of the bad."

The reference to Buddhism immediately suggests a very deep level of balance, where meditation and reflection put the very soul at ease. Organic foods not only purify the body, but soothe the mind, is what consumers were saying. The act of following an organic diet then takes on a powerful metaphysical meaning to consumers.

When participants spoke of poor diets, they used additive imagery, imagery that suggested heaviness: "loaded down," "polluted," and "saddled" to describe the type of imbalance they felt. When talking about organics, however, people used subtractive metaphors such as "cleansed," "purified," "lighter," "unburdened," and "free" to indicate the balanced state they experienced.

The Japanese firm is using this notion of subtractive ingredients to reframe its product in the United States. Originally, its messaging revolved around "juice with unique lactic processing." This stance would simply reinforce the idea that the naturally pure organic products had something artificially added in the juicing process, which thus contaminated them like any other "pollutant." Now, though, the company is framing its lactic processing as a subtraction issue—juice is processed *without* the high heat of conventional processing. This insight applied to all aspects of the product's positioning—name selection, packaging, advertising, and so on—and has made the product far more resonant with consumers.

Social Balance

Strong reciprocity is a term used to describe social balance. Strong reciprocity concerns the give-and-take actions found in cooperation, collaboration, and teamwork, and the more ephemeral benefits of conforming to social norms. So central is reciprocity, argues sociologist Herbert Gintis and his colleagues, that cultures that reward cooperation and punish failure to cooperate survive longer than do cultures in which these mechanisms are less well developed.[7]

Strong reciprocity is ultimately why consumers tend to patronize firms they perceive as having their best interests at heart. True consumer loyalty is an outcome of strong reciprocity, a balance process that keeps consumers in a sustained relationship with a firm or brand. Reciprocity is not necessarily achieved using so-called consumer loyalty programs.[8] Consumers do not want to feel as if they are being bought with explicit incentives, which may paradoxically diminish consumers' attachment to a specific company. As one participant in a brand loyalty study at Harvard's Mind of the Market Lab noted, "a rewards program is like we are mercenaries in a marketing war rather than volunteers." Instead, consumers will show and feel loyalty when they choose to reward a firm that, in turn, offers good value at a fair price.

Social responsibility concerning the environment is also understood through the lens of balance. This was evident in two independent multicountry studies that very closely mirrored one another. One study, for a consumer products firm, focused on consumers, and the other, for The World Bank, focused on executives. One balance theme common to both studies involved the balance between forces of nature. Nature was seen as a beautiful but destructive force. If nature isn't respected, it will strike back. "I fear nature's response," said one respondent. "The air is contaminated and global warming is the result of this contamination, and I think it is because the earth cannot bear it. I fear nature's response. Maybe that is why we have volcanic eruptions or tsunami."

Many consumers and executives felt a personal or corporate social responsibility, or both, to engage in environmentally friendly purchases and consumption behaviors. One person referring to a picture of soldiers in a parade commented, "As a citizen, I have a duty. So duty is why the military service came into mind. I usually do buy the environmental products or will act if I feel as though I have a duty to do it."

One reason consumers and executives are motivated to engage in socially responsible behaviors is to maintain balance over time. They feel they "owe it" to future generations: "They deserve to enjoy the same fresh air that I grew up with—not only for their enjoyment, but also for their health." Or, "I've got three sons and I'm a grandfather. That means you think ahead and know that the following generation should have a healthy environment."

Still, being socially responsible or balanced in one's consumption is not easy. Consumers compared the challenge of being environmentally friendly in their consumption behaviors to being on a diet. In some instances, they felt they should reduce their general consumption of certain products such as gasoline, and in other cases, the idea was to consume "healthier" products such as those made from recycled materials. Both practices involve discipline, effort, and sacrifice—doing things in moderation. Trying to lose weight and trying to protect the environment have uncertain and often distant outcomes. As with dieting, environmentally friendly consumption involves tasks that some people find so difficult and unpleasant they feel paralyzed and instead do nothing.

Moral Balance

Moral balance involves reciprocation, revenge, restitution, altruism, social indebtedness, and guilt. We hear it in phrases such as "He got what he deserved," "If I eat that pizza now, I'll pay for it later with indigestion," "She deserves better than that," "Life is not fair," "I should be allowed to smoke in public places if I want to," "Make love, not war," "Revenge is sweet," and "He who laughs last, lasts longest."

Moral balance underlies many beliefs and practices in religions that promise that current behaviors will be rewarded or punished in an afterlife. Interestingly, in directives to insure moral balance here and now on earth, the major religions all promote a variation on the Golden Rule, "Do unto others as you would have them do unto you."[9] Buddhism says, "Hurt not others in ways that you yourself would find hurtful." Judaism says, "What is hateful to you, do not to your fellow men." And Islam says, "No one of you is a believer until he desires for his brother that which he desires for himself."

Sometimes, moral balance or imbalance is intentionally private and no one else knows you are following the Golden Rule or repaying an institution. Some believe anonymous charitable donation is the highest type of generosity, because the giver expects nothing in return. Other times, doing one's part to help maintain the moral balance is quite open and public; for example, "It's my turn for the kids' soccer car pool," or even, "It's time to repay the favor you owe me." Likewise, community service can be performed as a voluntary, charitable deed or as a court-ordered way of helping to right a wrong.

Moral and social balance often combine in consumers' feelings of trust, or lack thereof, in particular brands, products, companies, and even industries. This is particularly likely for companies, institutions, and industries that consumers are very dependent on and that are perceived as large and well endowed with various kinds of resources. The pharmaceutical industry is a prime case in point.

Many consumers strongly feel that pharmaceutical companies must balance profits with ethical concerns. Consumers understand that pharmaceutical firms develop drugs that improve people's lives, as illustrated here: "I used to kayak and live in a houseboat. The pharmaceutical industry helps you so that you can still do some of that, despite age. There is medication if you have pain. That is the freedom of health."

At the same time, consumers feel that firms in this industry put profits over people. The idea of making "too much profit" is out of balance with the idea of a "helping industry." The image being referenced in the following quote is a cartoonish picture of a schoolteacher at her desk: "On one side of this old gray-haired schoolteacher, there is a boy with an apple, saying, 'Here I am; help me.' On the other side, there is a girl in ponytails holding a fistful of dollars, saying, 'I have a lot of money.' The schoolteacher is the pharmaceutical company."

To some extent, consumers understand that research justi-
fies drug pricing; pharmaceutical companies must have relatively higher prices for successful products to balance their
incurred costs on failed projects. One consumer described a picture of frogs she brought to her interview to represent her feelings about the pharmaceutical industry: "These frogs represent
the many choices of where to spend our money. It is a high-risk
business. You do not know how many projects fail, how many
actually produce useful drugs. There is price gouging, but they
can do it because they spent money on the research."

Consumers feel both empowered and trapped by pharmaceutical companies. On the positive side, people understand
that this industry helps improve and maintain health. High-
quality products contribute to the quality of life and allow the
user to feel more carefree. A sense of well-being made possible
by the medications leaves the consumer feeling free, in control,
relaxed, secure, optimistic, and able to enjoy the rewards of a
life of hard work. These feelings are more pronounced among
those who feel more trust in the pharmaceutical industry, as this
consumer does: "This gentleman, sitting with his dog in the
woods, is petting the dog which has a ball in his mouth. The
image represents peace of mind, going out, and doing what I
enjoy. What could be more peaceful, carefree, and relaxing?
The troubles of the world are taken care of."

These balance insights influenced all corporate communications and product-specific communications. As a result, the
pharmaceutical company could more effectively show consumers that it did a great deal of good through programs that
helped low-income families purchase medications and specific
other community outreach programs—programs that most people were unaware of.

Summary

Balance is one of the earliest deep metaphors that we develop. We start life with a basic grammar—a set of inborn capacities— for biological, mental, moral, and social balance. We also automatically experience the balancing functions of our physiological systems. Balance is one of the earliest manifestations of embodied cognition. As we progress in life, we acquire the sense of mental, social, and moral balance that are built on the physical balance system. Marketers should understand several aspects of balance:

- Balance is a fluid, not fixed, state.

- Consumers sometimes seek imbalance in a specific domain as part of a goal to seek an overall sense of balance. One consumer explained her involvement with extreme sports: "Sometimes you have to do crazy things to stay sane."

- Four types of balance could apply to a category and brand: physical balance, emotional balance, social balance, and moral balance.

- The four balance domains often spill over into one another. That is, balance in one domain can affect balance in the others.

- Leveraging multiple domains or extending consumer thinking to a new domain can increase consumer brand loyalty, as there are more sources of balance to meet the particular needs of a given situation.

4

Transformation

How Changes in Substance and Circumstances
Affect Consumer Thinking

Transformation involves an actual or contemplated change from one state to another. The changes may or may not be desired or planned. Nearly every product and service is evaluated in terms of the nature and magnitude of the change they foster or inhibit. An example is provided by Astorino, an architecture firm in Pittsburgh, charged with creating a $500 million state-of-the-art facility for the Children's Hospital of Pittsburgh. To better understand the needs of the hospital's end users, the firm conducted a study of patients, their parents, and the hospital staff. The study revealed that transformation was a key element of the hospital experience. Certainly, hospitals are about physical transformation (i.e., patients changing from sick to healed), but emotional transformations were common, too.

Staff, parents of patients, and especially the patients of the hospital all expressed being emotionally transformed by their hospital experiences. Some emotional transformations were positive (e.g., from an anxious to a calm state after a successful surgery), and some were negative (e.g., the feeling of isolation, being transplanted from one's home to a hospital for weeks on end). To acknowledge these important emotional themes, the architectural team has translated the deep metaphor of transformation into design elements. For instance, the team uses butterflies, an archetypical expression of transformation, in multiple areas of the building, including the primary entrance (figure I-3 in color insert). This corridor of butterfly images creates an immediate sense of transformation for everyone as he or she enters the hospital.

In addition, all the artwork chosen for the hospital expresses transformation. Near the elevator banks, designers are posting poems that feature transformational language derived from the interviews. The messages, meant to soothe and help people pass the time while waiting for the elevator to arrive, provide an optimistic feeling of transformation. These are just a few of the ways that the architects are incorporating deep metaphors into the hospital's design.

The Origins of Transformation As a Deep Metaphor

Transformation is a viewing lens for evaluating our bodies, thoughts, feelings, social relationships, and interactions with the physical world. An advertisement for CapitalOne leveraged the classic transformational, fairy-tale kiss in which a beautiful princess attempts to transform a frog and a succession of other creatures into a rich prince. Her failed attempt to assume the magician archetype provides attention-getting humor. Myths, fairy tales, and stories help us make sense of change in our lives. Think of *Dr. Jekyll and Mr. Hyde*, in which one man changes between two distinct personalities, or *Frankenstein*, in which an experiment to transform a dead body to a human being creates a monster instead. Or there is Franz Kafka's famous story, *Metamorphoses*, in which an ordinary man wakes up one morning—as a cockroach. Numerous Biblical stories of plagues, floods, and miracles involve dramatic transformations.[1] We view people, events, and objects in terms of changes between past, present, and future states, and sometimes we even focus on the lack of change. Paradoxically, the human penchant for noticing differences is one factor that makes transformation a universal viewing lens.

In *Marketing Metaphoria*, we use the term *transformation* rather than *change* to emphasize the more profound character of the changes that this deep metaphor addresses. Transformations may be fully anticipated or a complete surprise, desired or dreaded, gradual or abrupt, slow or fast. For example, people enroll in continuing education courses because they seek or anticipate an eventual career transformation. A variety of goods and services, such as warrantees, insurance policies, wills, and other legal contracts, can help a person plan for unwelcome and often unanticipated transformations due to product failure, crime, accident, or death. We may climb the corporate ladder in a decade, only to lose our job in a day. We protest rapid technological upgrades, as simple as when The Coca-Cola Company attempted to replace "classic" Coke with "new" Coke. Not only was the product formulation transformed, but consumers were unable to get the physical and emotional transformations from "new" Coke that they got from "classic" Coke.

The *absence of transformation* is also part of this frame. When anticipated change does not occur, we may be relieved or disturbed. We are relieved when our firm is unaffected by a recession or when we remain healthy during an outbreak of the flu. We are disappointed when "new and improved" products or services perform no better than "old" ones, when a new management team cannot effect needed organizational changes, when surgery is unsuccessful, or when either the implementation of an innovation or an organization's growth occurs more slowly than planned.

Consider these expressions concerning the body, mind, and social contexts:

- "She has trimmed down."

- "She is starting to walk."

- "He has not aged a day."

- "You have convinced me."

- "She is so moody."

- "My attitude has evolved."

- "The old way of life is gone."

- "Nothing ever happens around here."

- "Their political agenda has grown radical."

- "We are ridding the world of disease and hunger."

All these statements involve change. Transformation as a deep metaphor for thinking about and reacting to events, places, and objects has its origins in several spheres of life. As a viewing lens, transformation is an important by-product of the many experiences that drive our physical, mental, and social development. For example, one of the basic drives people have is a need to learn or to know.[2] Children, for example, have an innate curiosity that drives a desire to learn—and this desire is necessary for survival. Conscious and unconscious learning is one of the most profound transformations of mind that we can experience. For adults, for example, learning how to master the Internet, delegate authority, or tango serves other important needs related to self-actualization and social dominance.

Transformation is evident in our personal stories, too. Ordinary people play the lottery hoping to become instant millionaires; consumers of all ages buy cosmetics to paint themselves more attractive; as audiences, we allow make-believe to become real when we watch slapstick comedy, horror films, and soap operas, which transform our emotional states and cause us to laugh, be frightened, or cry. Organizations are transformed through growth, shake-ups, mergers, and bankruptcy.[3] Cultures change as they come into contact with other value systems or as new technologies take hold.[4]

The Transformation Lens

Transformation may be the most pervasive deep metaphor among consumers. Nearly all goods and services are intended to facilitate or retard passage from one state to another. This makes transformation a potentially relevant viewing lens for most offerings. Moreover, transformations that seem to be unique to the mind, body, or society often spill over into other aspects of life.[5] A transformational external event such as a natural disaster or

civil war can transform family relationships, increase suscepti-
bility to illness, alter personal values, change attitudes toward
particular ethnic groups, and do much, much more.

A consumer in a study on leisure-time activities described
the mental change she experienced when she was physically detached from her everyday surroundings. Referring to a picture
of someone dealing with a dead car battery in a snowy parking
lot, she commented, "On holiday, I leave my emotional bag-
gage behind. I switch off. I just enjoy life. When I come back,
life looks better. It gives me strength to be more confident, to
forget problems. On holiday, you're totally detached; you can
regenerate. My battery is recharged."

Sometimes, significant transformations, even those we long
for, are bittersweet. The Cheerios brand team wanted to understand how mothers feel about the transitions that their children
go through (since some of the transitions have implications for
nutrition and mealtime experiences). Many mothers made comments like the following: "When his first tooth fell out, we cele-
brated. But when the Tooth Fairy went to put money under
his pillow, I had tears in my eyes—we were losing more than a
tooth." Insights like this were used in advertising to show an understanding of the paradox and conflicts parents feel as their
children grow up.

Some changes are inconsequential. Another inch of snow in
Vermont is unlikely to be noticed. The presence or absence of
other changes, however, may be very consequential and felt
deeply. For example, a heartburn sufferer who found an effective treatment felt profoundly transformed: "When the treatment actually worked, I felt like a knight slaying a dragon. I was
no longer the victim of a fire-breathing monster." The pharmaceutical firm involved in the study is now developing point-of-

purchase displays depicting consumers as conquerors instead of victims. Seemingly small events, such as eating potato chips, washing your car, or using gift-wrap paper can produce noteworthy, albeit brief, transformations in our feelings. In a study about keeping car exteriors clean, many drivers expressed transformation themes, despite knowing that no material transformation had occurred beyond the car's appearance: "Whenever I clean my car, it runs better and even faster. I know that makes no sense and sounds silly. Cleanliness cannot make a difference. But it really does. I can feel it."

In another study, consumers spoke about how hair care products transform their appearance. In evaluating one shampoo brand, the participants used the primary deep metaphor of transformation, but for another brand, they used the deep metaphor of control. That is, consumers viewed the first brand in terms of how it made hair brighter and the second brand in terms of how it made hair more manageable. These insights enabled the firm that was conducting the research to reposition its two brands in terms of transformation (brand 1) and control (brand 2), putting appropriate transformation and control cues in various communications, including package design. The firm is now identifying relevant deep metaphors to use for positioning a new product formulation that provides both benefits.

Sometimes, the inability to transform can be a powerful viewing lens. In a study evaluating new advertisements for a leading weight management product, consumers spoke about the challenges of gaining and losing weight, which are physical transformations. They described their feelings about these transformations and used such pictures as a huge container ship, elephants, pencils, a magician, a feather, the Hoover Dam, a Bible, and a person leaping over several buses while on a motorcycle.

One consumer described her failed attempts at weight loss: "At first, I thought I would end up looking like a pencil, but I eventually concluded I am and will always be a freighter." However, transformation as a viewing lens for her past efforts became even more evident in her skepticism about the test advertisements: "It would take an act of God for me to experience what that advertisement promises." In this case, the perceived impossibility of a transformation influenced her judgments of the product. Another person with a similarly unsuccessful history of dieting revealed his skepticism: "Only a skinny person, light as a feather, could think up that message." For these people, the deep metaphor of transformation, specifically their perceived inability to transform their weight, rooted in past failures, is a dominant filter for viewing claims about weight-loss programs. The company reevaluated its existing communications in light of these insights and formulated a new creative brief, focusing on what people think is realistically feasible.

Shopping As a Transformative Experience

Shopping can involve different transformations, some negative, some positive. In shopping studies around the globe, we have found that consumers share similar views about the transformational consequences of their shopping journeys. For example, shopping is seen to have an alchemizing quality, whereby "magical" alterations in moods, self-esteem, relationships, and bodies occur. The positive, enhancing transformations involve emotional states that shift from stress to relaxation; physical states that shift from fatigue to energy; and social relationships that make a person feel closer to friends. One consumer said, "Shopping can add color to an otherwise black-and-white day. It gives you pleasure and takes you out of the bad mood you are in. You might be upset, so you shop to cheer yourself up or to reward yourself." Another commented, "Shopping by myself brings relaxation. It is just being by yourself, looking at different things, seeing things you would like to have, and finding things to make the house prettier. It is relaxing because you are around other people even if you don't know them."

Shopping's positive emotional results are joy, relaxation, and feeling rewarded or even proud when an unexpected bargain on a long-sought item is found. Going shopping can be a momentary escape that leads to an emotional transformation.

The products and services consumers buy for themselves may be intended to bring about transformation. They may bring positive physical or emotional changes that help consumers to feel happier, inspired, or more stimulated. Some examples of deep dives into the basic motivation to go shopping for particular experiences include the following:

- The Coca-Cola Company's exploration of the transformative meanings of "feel good"

- Work by Hallmark and Eastman Kodak Company to understand the transformative role memories play in people's lives

- Motorola's investigation of what it means to feel secure in otherwise threatening circumstances

- The World Bank's study of how youth envision their future

- Procter & Gamble's study of the meaning of becoming clean and germfree

Studies like these yield fundamental insights into a deep human experience that makes specific goods and services relevant. These insights, explored during workable wondering sessions, have powerful strategic and tactical marketing implications. They enable firms to develop new ways of engaging the experience of feeling good, develop leadership training programs for young adults, and create products and services that help consumers keep track of memorable events. Managers are better able to seamlessly integrate product attributes and their functional consequences with consumers' social and emotional needs and personal values and goals.

Well-Being As Transformation

The human body is often compared to a machine. When the machine becomes "run down" by sickness or stress, it needs to be repaired. Dealing with such repairs often invokes physical and emotional transformation themes, as was discussed briefly in the Children's Hospital of Pittsburgh example. Our bodies can also feel "broken" when we are stressed and overwhelmed by daily chores. In a study about the use of a personal trainer, participants spoke about feeling "dirty" and in need of "repair" as a motivation for hiring a trainer. After their sessions, they said they felt cleansed, invigorated, at ease, quietly proud, and more connected to themselves.

Sleep is one of the major transformations of daily life. Out of biological necessity, we nightly transform from conscious to unconscious states, and every morning, we transform back again. For many reasons, sleep disorders are deeply disturbing. An independent advertisement evaluation of the award-winning ad campaign by Sepracor for the sleep aid Lunesta identified transformation as the primary deep metaphor operating among consumers who were viewing the ad.

In the ads, a luna moth plays a critical role in activating the idea of transformation. While the naming of the product and the use of the luna moth were meant to suggest nighttime peace associated with the moon, most people failed to identify the luna moth by its proper name. Instead, they saw a more familiar butterfly. The transformations people associate with butterflies—larva to cocoon to butterfly—were what made the campaign so effective. In the television ad, the butterfly touches the consumer, who is lying awake in bed. And like the classic transformational kiss from a princess that turns a frog into a prince, the insomniac is transformed from a state of wakefulness into a state of peaceful slumber. Referring to a butterfly's developmental stages, one person commented, "If only we could go to sleep as naturally as the butterfly does its thing, that would be wonderful."

Another person, invoking the princess and the frog, said, "I've taken the medication, and I feel the butterfly's touch almost right away and I'm reminded of the story my mother used to read to me about a princess saving a prince by kissing a frog. The pill is the princess. It changes me. It saves me from lying awake. It's a kiss of sorts."

The butterfly is a visual metaphor for the medication and an icon of transformation. The specific deep metaphor themes that surfaced in this study involve safe transformations, restful transformations, natural transformations, and even magical transformations.

Escape As Transformation

Visiting amusement parks and theme restaurants can be transformational experiences. For example, to increase sales of Mickey

Mouse and related paraphernalia, the Walt Disney Company wanted to understand how people related to the famous mouse. The firm undertook a study among adults about both their childhood memories and their adult impressions of Mickey Mouse. Mickey's essence—his goodness, fairness, and openness; his protective and caring nature; and his clever, impish character—makes him a truly beloved figure. He has become a central part of growing up and even growing old. It was discovered that this fictional character had transformational effects so profound that people were willing to spend large sums of money on Mickey Mouse paraphernalia as a way of transporting themselves back to more idyllic times and sharing those times with their children. This was important partly because parents wanted to create for their children similar experiences that would provide therapeutic value when the children became adults. Mickey Mouse provides a safety zone of memories that we can enjoy repeatedly and create anew for our children. He has a magical quality, one that enables adults to feel transported to a fantasy world that renews and refreshes them, physically and mentally, even if only briefly. One consumer explained, "As a child, I would think that he was real. But, now, I would be like, 'I know there is a person in that suit,' but it would still bring me back to the childlike state." Even Mickey himself went through a transformation, from his early images as a shifty-looking Steamboat Willy in a 1928 cartoon to the cute, neotenic (open, baby-face look) creature known worldwide today.

One of the most powerful transformations Mickey Mouse engenders is allowing adults to feel like a child again. Consumers expressed this fountain-of-youth theme in various ways, such as "He brings back memories of childhood and that excitement you feel when you're a child. We all need that once in a while. Kind of a refresher course in being young again," and "He gives us license to do all those things that you did as a child, and not feel ridiculous."

Transformative experiences that bring us to another time or place are also provided by the arts, say, attending a ballet or playing the guitar. The arts help us move from everyday worries and stress to a state of lessened anxieties and relief from work or home life pressures. The arts enable us to reengage past hopes and feelings, transport us into the future by allowing us to imagine our personal growth or development, and offer us different viewpoints and understanding. In a study for the Heinz Endowments for the Arts, one consumer described her experience: "The arts take you away from your everyday existence. You feel a release from the tension of every day. I don't feel closed in. I feel freedom, and it also has a calming effect. Whether it is a movie, dance, or looking at a picture, you're suddenly in a new world and come back refreshed with a smile on your face." Throughout this study, people from many walks of life commented on a variety of art forms and described how the arts changed them by providing increased energy, calmness, relaxation, and an improved ability to think, all of which led to greater achievement and raised self-esteem. People expressed feelings of excitement, youthfulness, and escape, which led to feelings of freedom and a loss of inhibitions.

In another study, the League of Broadway Theatre Owners and Producers found that attending Broadway plays could expand consumers' understanding of views other than their own. One consumer said, "Everyone gets something different from it. There is always a benefit to seeing something in a different way. Otherwise we take things for granted. We assume things about people that we shouldn't. It broadens your horizons." Another explained, "I always look for similarities between myself and people who I don't think necessarily would be similar to me. When you broaden your horizons, you can more easily see what others have to offer and what you have in common with other people."

Sports have much in common with other performing arts. Marketing authorities such as Irving Rein, Philip Kotler, and Ben Shields have framed the challenge for sports marketers to increase audience engagement in terms of transformation.[6] Separately, a study conducted for Major League Baseball identified the transformational power of baseball-related memories for many baseball fans. For example, one fan said, "Baseball has made a huge difference in my life. As a kid when things were bad at home, I always had players I could look up to and imagined what it would be like if one of them was my father. Other times, I would just think that I could do what they do if I tried hard. That inspired me. Now, when things are crappy at home or at work, I just go to a game. Being there brings back these memories."

Identity Transformation

Our self-identity, our sense of who we are, often changes as past experience merges with current experience. One increasingly common example in today's global world involves moving from one country to another. Not only do those who move experience major change, but so, too, do their children born in the new country. Consequently, very interesting instances of self-identity and transformation occur among these so-called second-generation citizens. British subjects of Pakistani heritage may have different transformational experiences than do Brazilian citizens with Italian backgrounds. All these people, however, will share certain experiences in adjusting to the country of citizenship while maintaining important identities with familial and cultural heritage. These transitions are not always smooth. They may involve ambivalence and struggle as certain changes are resisted and others eagerly sought.

One of our studies focused on what it is like to be a second-generation Hispanic in the United States today.[7] Regardless of gender or parental country of origin, all consumers in this study wrestled with the transformations involved in bringing two cultural identities—their parents' and that of their own countries of birth—into alignment. This concern clearly expresses the deep metaphor of balance as well as transformation.

The creation of a personal identity is complex.[8] In this study, consumers expressed a number of transformation-laden themes: the paradox of blending two traditions while also keeping elements of them separate and the challenges of managing different expectations, coping with stereotypes, and balancing internal needs with external constraints. Some of these themes appear in figure 4-1.

The story behind the image reveals a number of thoughts and feelings about making certain changes while resisting others, such as the need to develop independence and self-reliance; the importance of learning; struggles to achieve and become competitive; the importance of maintaining roots as a source of continuity (e.g., food traditions and choice of husband); the fear or anxiety that change can produce (see especially the people holding masks over their faces); the burden that stereotypes add to the task of fitting in; the challenge of learning a new language; and the special satisfaction derived when the transformations

Figure 4-1: Identity Transformation

"The independent woman with the scarf on her head resembles me, how I like to be independent. On the other side is an African American woman, athletic and competitive. I am that, too, determined to be the best that I can be as an Hispanic in the United States. The island of my roots is isolated, but so much still comes from there, like that Hispanic man, and I want to stay within my roots when I get married.

"In the distance are people who left the island. Hiding behind masks, they feel scared of not fitting in or being welcomed. The golden award opposite the independent woman means that we should continue achieving different goals in our lives. Finally, the hardworking man on a mule or a horse means that we must work extra hard outside our country because we must fit in.

"As an Hispanic and American, I see myself open to a variety of opportunities from both sides. I know the American way and I relate to an Hispanic way. I can fit in to an American place and I can fit into a Spanish place."

are balanced, allowing one to be in both a Hispanic "place" and an American "place."

In keeping both a Hispanic and an American identity, the consumer who made this image gives herself two options. In a Hispanic environment, she can transform into a Hispanic persona. In an American environment, she can transform into an American persona. Either way, she can feel accepted. This ability to shift between cultures gives her power. The narrator sees great prospects in her future and approaches the world with confidence.

Other discoveries in this study involved striking a balance between what one could lose and what one could gain with a transformation. Many second-generation Hispanics face the challenge of retaining sufficient cultural identity associated with their parents' origins while succeeding in a different cultural milieu.

Most people in this study mentioned various goods and services—from food products to entertainment—that enabled them to be in both places. Of particular interest was a dislike of advertising and entertainment programming content that appeared insincere or inauthentic in attempting to appeal to Hispanic identity. These were seen as false products that only heightened the conflict of dual identities rather than making a dual heritage a source of rich satisfaction and even pride. Knowing how this segment of the population felt—and, more importantly, hoped to feel in the future—about their heritage was crucial for several companies in creating meaningful storybooks for children, unique personal albums and "journey logs" as gifts for parents and for other second generation Hispanics, and even special travel-related services.

Summary

Many transformative experiences characterize our lives, and our physical survival and interpersonal success depend on our managing important changes effectively. The presence or absence of transformation and the qualities of past, present, and future transformations create a viewing lens that serves as a powerful, automatic, and unconscious way of evaluating experience.

Throughout the chapter, we have made several observations about transformation:

- Transformations can be physical, social, or mental, and sometimes even all three.

- Transformation in one sphere of life often spills over into other spheres. For example, we view physical transformations in terms of the emotional and interpersonal transformations they may trigger, and vice versa.

- The broad range of transformations in life—from shopping to personal trainers to Mickey Mouse to sleep aids—is a testament to the power of this deep metaphor.

Virtually all products and services are tied to transformation. Some products cause the transformation (e.g., drinking coffee for physical transformation), while other products and services are used before or after a transformation to note its occurrence (e.g., a graduation gift).

5

Journey

How the Meeting of Past, Present, and Future
Affects Consumer Thinking

O ur sense of the past, present, and future often combine to create the experience of a physical, social, or psychological journey. This combination serves as a major viewing lens for all manner of experiences. One of the largest residential real estate companies in the United States recently began worrying about the marked drop-off in inquiries among potential first-time home buyers. The trend was partly national, influenced by well-publicized economic factors. From its previous research, however, the firm knew that more than strict economics was influencing consumer behavior. Before relaunching a mortgage insurance product, managers needed a deeper understanding of the social and psychological bases for the financial drivers. A research team interviewed young couples across the country who were considering a first-time home purchase. One Minneapolis couple jointly created the image in figure I-4 (color insert).

Many thoughts and feelings bubbled up for the woman, and there was more than a little tension between the two as they created this image. For her, a terrible past experience introduced great anxiety as she thought of buying her first home, and she clearly dragged this childhood experience along on her journey toward home ownership. On the other hand, the diving board with the dollar signs on it represented her husband's view that their first new home would be a "springboard to a really nice big home when we have children." Clearly, they were experiencing the same journey differently. The wife approached it with more fear and trepidation than her husband did.

Among all the couples, at least one partner expressed both anxiety and optimism about buying a first home. Typically, both partners had these mixed emotions. The causes and manifestations of these feelings differed from person to person and couple to couple. In all cases, however, the participants' past experiences, present circumstances, and envisioned futures merged to create a social, psychological, and financial journey—a combination that serves as a major viewing lens for all manner of physical and emotional experiences. The first home represents a significant milestone activating prior and future aspects of this journey. However, the real estate company focused on the common ground that couples shared: the need for protection as they continued onward. In this example, the wife saw the insurance product as a cushion for her fears and for her husband, "should his springboard break." Appealing to each couple's need for protection on this scary journey proved a successful marketing strategy for the mortgage insurance product. The real estate firm learned how to position its product so that it aligned with the important goals and values of these young couples.

The Origins of Journey As a Deep Metaphor

When asked to write a brief story about either a crinkled or smooth piece of paper, almost everyone—from third-graders to senior executives—chooses the crinkled paper. That is because the crinkles imply a history, the paper's curious journey from smooth origins to a creased present. From missions to outer space to a quick trip to the convenience store, journeys large and small engage our attention.

Journeys also frame our desires, from shopping at the mall to pursuing our career. Is our life's journey brief or long? A sprint or a marathon? Exciting or tedious? It all depends on whom you ask, when you ask, and the context of your question. How we frame time and unfolding events—the essence of the deep metaphor *journey*—influences such consumer decisions as home buying, financial planning, charitable giving, health care, snacks, and vacations, to name a few.

A consumer who risks inheriting a disease in his forties and one whose parents are vibrant octogenarians may make different health-care choices. The personal financial planning of a twenty-year-old consumer who believes "life is short" may differ entirely from that of a forty-year-old who believes "a lot of life remains ahead." Two consumers with equal debt may save differently, depending on their past success in managing similar debt.

A few dynamics establish journey as a deep metaphor when we engage in daily living. Our consciousness, sense of time, notions of cause and effect, use of the remembered past to plan or imagine the future, and concept of an afterlife often employ the metaphor of journey.

Our awareness of time distinguishes us from all other species. Rather than rely exclusively on instinct, we apply past experiences and current circumstances when planning our future. This past-present-future sensibility grounds journey as a deep metaphor.[1] It relates to the evolution of consciousness, that is, our well-developed awareness of awareness.[2] How we view our past and how we approach our future shape our self-identities. The emergence of self-identity is a complex process. A consumer who spent summers in a vacation house on the shore may aspire for his children to experience the same. Another consumer, who spent every summer sweltering in a one-room apartment in the inner city, may also aspire for his children to spend summers in a vacation house on the shore. To complicate matters, yet another consumer, who spent childhood summers sweltering in a one-room apartment in the inner city, may aspire to raising her children in a spacious suburban duplex with central air-conditioning—and spend time in the summer with grandparents in the city. The central point remains this: our awareness of time and the unfolding of related events and their consequences insures that who we were and who we want to be influences our understanding of who we are now.[3] Often unconsciously, we view our identities and our choices through the deep metaphor of journey.

Neuroscientists know that specific brain sites are active when we sense time moving whether quickly or slowly.[4] Our sense of cause and effect involves the sensation of time and the perception of unfolding events, which further adds to our use of journey as a viewing lens.[5] For example, when we see a video in which one billiard ball is striking another, we expect the second ball to move ahead immediately on impact. However, should a small delay occur in the second ball's movement, we are surprised: the second ball's expected "journey" was interrupted. Were the ball to move at a right angle when we expected it to move straight ahead, we experience even greater surprise because the journey not only was interrupted but also followed an unexpected path.

What Journeys Reveal About Consumers

The expressed specifics of a journey can provide marketers with powerful clues into consumers' minds. For instance, the journey themes that consumers use have considerable strategic relevance. Notice the difference between two very similar statements:

- "I am fast approaching my retirement date."

- "My retirement date is fast approaching."

The first stresses a theme of agency: the person moves toward a specific event or point in time. The second reveals an objectified theme: the event moves toward the person. Both involve a journey, but marketers must understand whether consumers identify with the mover (subject, actor) or the moved (object, acted on).[6]

After analyzing different journey themes, one financial services firm segmented new client accounts according to whether the prospects viewed themselves or their retirement date as the moving subject. The firm then developed two different presentations of the same financial product to the two segments. This dual strategy increased new accounts in *both* segments and decreased the time in obtaining the accounts. Similarly, the insurance company Nationwide adopted the moving-object approach. In its campaign "Life comes at you fast," Nationwide stressed how life's events can blindside you, and so you should prepare for them. Usually, consumers view approaching events with more urgency than they do events being approached, especially when the impending events involve financial obligations. In other words, we consider retirement a controllable event when we see it as a milestone on the road of life (an approached event) rather than as a speed demon bearing down on us (an approaching event). So, to establish healthy relationships with consumers, companies must understand how people frame their journeys.

Which Consumer Should You Target?

Imagine yourself a successful financial planner with an almost full client list. You meet with two prospective clients, knowing that you can accept only one. Both in their late forties, they live in upper-middle-class suburbs with their spouse and children and have roughly the same amount of money to invest.

The first prospect, Mr. Kumar, is affable and enthusiastic with a positive outlook on life. He uses such phrases as "Life is short" and "You're only on this earth for a short time," and he wants "no regrets" when he "looks back on life." The second prospect, Mrs. Li, seems quite pleasant though more reserved. She uses such phrases as "have a lot of life left" and retirement will be "the beginning of a new life" rather than the "end of a journey."

Which prospect should you take on? Clearly, Mrs. Li, because her metaphors signal a savings orientation. You can tell that she has a long-term-investment mind-set and understands her own need for money to start her new life. Mr. Kumar, with his "live day-to-day" mind-set, will more likely spend his money today. These few seemingly superficial expressions reveal a lot about a potential customer's—or an employee's—frame of mind and can thus inform your decisions about pursuing and communicating with that person.

Now imagine yourself a car salesperson. Rather than return to his office, Mr. Kumar visits your Lexus dealership next to the financial planner's office. After assessing Mr. Kumar's life views, you quickly realize that you have met your dream customer. After all, who better to buy a luxury car than someone who values spending more than saving? You reinforce his views, "Mr. Kumar, you live only once, right?"

Marketers of many luxury or "big-ticket" items know that their consumers make purchase decisions with this frame of mind.[7] Why else would consumers pay $250 for a pair of designer jeans, when they could purchase an almost identical pair for $50? They enjoy life's journey by treating themselves along the way, and through their conspicuous consumption, they communicate to others that their journey is very special.

Journey Themes That Speak to Consumers

Marketers often leverage three journey themes—known or unknown outcomes, obstacles and facilitators, and the ups and downs of journeys—but could do so more effectively by engaging the emotions tied to each theme. Anticipation, for example, is a primary emotion often relevant to known journeys while surprise is a primary emotion active when on unknown journeys.

Known Journeys

Although all journeys typically involve destinations, we may or may not know their outcomes. Consider these journeys:

- Taking a one-week cruise to the Caribbean

- Going to college to obtain a degree

- Making a monthly mortgage payment on a home

- Doing the weekly grocery shopping

A cynic may argue that nothing is certain—a person may drop out of college, miss a payment, and so on. However, at the outset of some journeys, consumers *think* they know how the journey will end; they have a clear goal and end state in mind. For this reason, a journey that veers off course and has a surprise ending can create quite an emotional impact—and the mortgage insurance product described at the beginning of this chapter appeals to "travelers" who fear an unpleasant detour. Known journeys can have positive or negative outcomes. In journeys with positive outcomes, the consumer focuses on reaching the goal. For example, a credit card owner repeatedly uses the card to accumulate points toward the goal of a free air ticket. For journeys with negative outcomes, the traveler typically procrastinates or avoids a destination if possible. For instance, someone with high blood pressure knows that if he or she keeps on the present "track," the result may be a stroke. This realization may launch another journey—seeking medical treatment and changing a lifestyle. How consumers use journey to frame their thoughts and feelings can differ greatly. For example, some consumers may feel proud of their facial wrinkles (as one person in a cosmetics study put it, "I've earned them!") and avoid skin care products; others may feel shame and seek plastic surgery. In a study of all terrain vehicle (ATV) purchases, one man referred to his ATV as "my emotional getaway car" while his wife described it as a "guaranteed trip to the emergency room."

Nearly everyone is familiar with the De Beers Group's "A diamond is forever" campaign, which leverages the notion of constancy in a timeless journey. Patek Philippe has also established a strong, lasting bond with its consumers by using the deep metaphor of journey in its advertising. Its campaigns regularly feature themes that emphasize establishing a legacy for future generations (e.g., "Begin your own tradition"). More recently, the company used the tagline "You never actually own a Patek Philippe. You merely look after it for the next generation," wherein the watch—and not the consumer—is traveling across generations. Its owners are privileged waypoints in the heirloom's journey.

Unknown Journeys

Journeys with unknown outcomes often feature excitement or anxiety, depending on whether the outcomes are positive or negative. Consider these journeys:

- Buying a home for the first time

- Searching for a job

- Attempting to quit smoking after several failures

- Gambling in Las Vegas

- Discovering and then switching brands

- Skydiving for the first time

This last example may seem like a known journey—odds are that the person will land safely—but the small chance of the parachute's not opening creates excitement. A key difference between known and unknown journeys is control. In a positive unknown journey—such as a sky dive—the consumer seeks a momentary loss of control to experience excitement "at the mercy of the parachute." Similarly, sports fans watch games not to see their team win but to see their team have a chance to win. The fans desire the thrill and excitement of an uncertain outcome that relies on the up-and-down scoring until the very end.

Many consumers purposefully embark on unknown consumption journeys. When consumers discover a "hidden gem" of a restaurant, spend thousands of dollars for "adventure travel," or test-drive a sports car, they experience a variety of emotions: fear of the unknown, initial anxiety and excitement, and reward and satisfaction, or loss and disappointment. Just as famous historical explorers turned unknown expeditions into known ones by sharing their journals, maps, or travelogues, consumers share their discoveries with their friends. We reduce our friends' fears and heighten their anticipation by promising them, "Trust me, I've been there and the meal will be amazing!" Thus, even messages have their own journey through buzz or word of mouth.

On life's journey, we crave control over our bodies, minds, and resources. Regaining or maintaining control matters greatly to us in unknown journeys, especially if we view the journey as negative, as with failing health. Research on health issues as simple as heartburn or as complex as late-stage cancer demonstrates that patients overwhelmed by illness no longer feel in control of their life's journey, a very frightening experience. For example, before developing diabetes, people felt that they were directing their life's journey. After their diagnosis, they felt as if the disease was "in the driver's seat." These findings teach marketers to position medication as a resource for getting "back behind the wheel" in their journey.

In separate projects relating to parenthood and child rearing, consumers' expressions reveal obvious journey elements. For this reason, marketers should leverage this deep metaphor in product positioning and communications strategies targeting parents. Various companies have used similar journey insights differently:

- A baby-food company positions itself as a resource for mothers who are looking for answers to nutrition questions on their motherhood journey.

- An athletic-apparel company provides expert advice on getting back into shape in the weeks and months following childbirth.

- A baby-products retailer's communications empathized with the overwhelming—albeit exciting and enjoyable—unknowns that mothers-to-be will experience.

- A hospital repositioned itself as the ideal companion and resource during and after childbirth—to ensure the baby's good beginning on its life's journey.

Obstacles and Facilitators on Consumer Journeys

Some journeys are inherently more difficult than others. Shopping for a new car is less difficult than overcoming cancer, but more difficult than choosing picture-frame hangers. All journeys can become harder or easier, depending on the obstacles and

facilitators along the way. The following journey-invoking surface metaphors reflect the salience of obstacles and facilitators:

Obstacles

- "He had to overcome many hurdles to achieve success."

- "That was just a bump in the road in this relationship."

- "You are on a slippery slope."

- "We hit a brick wall in our negotiations."

- "I am stuck in my career."

Facilitators

- "Let us bridge the gap in our thinking."

- "They extended a helping hand during my recovery."

- "Those ahead of me paved the way for my success."

- "Coffee fuels me throughout the day."

Virtually any product or service facilitates consumers' journeys. American Express advises its customers, "Don't leave
home without it," the "it" being the American Express card.
About its own credit card and its consumers' journeys, Visa
says, "It's everywhere you want to be." Other products enhance
a journey differently, as an iPod does in one's commute to work.
When talking about their iPods, especially their life without
one, consumers use such vivid language as "like an emergency
exit door got blocked," "impoverished," "wander aimlessly," and
"I would arrive at work in a very bad mood every day." Apple

used such insights to position the iPod as a supportive traveling companion, not simply as an entertainment system.

Obstacles may frustrate or anger us until we—or some facilitators—remove or overcome them. Products and services are typically those journey facilitators. For example, cars that are more fuel-efficient help consumers overcome the hurdle of high gas prices as they manage their resources. In modern Western society, consumers often look negatively on aging. Consequently, a plethora of products and services promises to help consumers slow down, hide, or stop the aging process. One company markets a product line with the slogan "instant age rewind" to suggest that the product can reverse or at least slow down the journey. Some consumers have a positive view of aging, because it brings freedom. In a study of romance-novel readers, one consumer said, "One of the benefits of getting older is that I do not care as much what people think. I can say and do what I would not have when I was much younger."

The language consumers use provides clues to their perceived obstacles and facilitators. In an interview regarding finances, one consumer told us, "It was all smooth sailing in the late nineties; we were just cruising along, enjoying the ride. Then the dot-com crash hit us like a tidal wave. We tried to navigate the rough waters, but in the end, we hit rock bottom." This financial journey began pleasantly, but quickly turned hazardous as obstacles arose during the dot-com crash. The consumer could not find anything to help smooth the journey, which ended in failure. A luckier—or more financially savvy—person experienced the dot-com crash differently: "As soon as the water started getting rough, I was advised to change course, to follow a more conservative investment path. I shifted more to other tools, such as CDs and saving bonds as a buffer for my-self. So I came out of it relatively unscathed."

The metaphors here focus on facilitators—advice, tools, and buffers—for enduring a tough time. In fact, many financial advertisements seen on TV today incorporate these specific visual metaphors. The ads show images of passengers navigating sail-boats in a fog-laden ocean, lighthouses and other beacons in the distance, and a safe harbor. Consumers understand the messages because of the familiar frames.

Love and other relationships are also major journeys. The Diamond Trading Company, the marketing arm of De Beers Group, launched a major campaign based on research on what men experience when giving diamonds to their partners.[8] The journey theme's prominence gave De Beers the confidence to call its latest design series "The Journey Collection." The designs involved a graduated pattern of movement from smaller to larger diamonds. The $20 million advertising campaign (along with substantially more financial investment from retailers) uses journey metaphors as well, including the tagline "With every step, love grows."

Uphill and Downhill Journeys

Sir Winston Churchill described life as a journey: "Every day you may make progress. Every step may be fruitful. Yet there will stretch out before you an ever-lengthening, ever-ascending, ever-improving path. You know you will never get to the end of the journey. But this, so far from discouraging, only adds to the joy and glory of the climb." Churchill pointed out that life is not easy, that it is an uphill, "ever-ascending" path. He told us, however, to focus on the "glory of the climb," a phrase that resonated with the public, most of whom have physically experienced uphill climbs.

Uphill journeys typically feature difficulties and struggle and can be emotionally daunting. The outcome at the top of the journeys, however, can bring great reward and a sense of achievement. Emotionally, uphill journeys may seem daunting, but as the journey nears its destination, the consumer is filled with happiness, anticipation, and, finally, a sense of triumph.

Downhill journeys can have both positive and negative connotations. The idea of descent can imply heading toward a lower, undesired, or less successful physical, socioeconomic, or emotional state from some previous pinnacle, as when someone says, "My health really went downhill from there," or "Smoking is a slippery slope." Descriptions consumers use when talking about a negative downhill journey are "downward spiral," "runaway train," or "sinking ship." But the downhill metaphor can be positive when consumers have overcome some initially difficult obstacle and the remaining journey seems easy. In this instance, one says positively, "It is all downhill from here," or "The rest is smooth sailing," meaning that everything will be fine. Positive downhill journey metaphors appear in "I am over the hump," or "Now I can coast." One home buyer used a picture of a skier holding a trophy near the foot of a ski jump to express her sense of having completed one phase of her journey: "Victory in finding just what I wanted after traipsing through house after house. I am sure the skier had his doubts, but is thinking right now, 'That was an exciting run down.'"

Many important journeys have both uphill and downhill elements. Our relationships—be they business partnerships, marriages, or friendships—all have their "ups and downs" and "peaks and valleys" and can be filled with "a rollercoaster of emotions."

When we get through the downs, we are able to enjoy the ups so much more; in fact, some people are convinced that they need the lows to enjoy the highs. This viewpoint helps some to cope, survive, and ultimately succeed on their journeys. Marriage vows contain the well-known phrase "for better or for worse" to "warn" both parties that their journey together will not always be easy, thus preparing them for a long-term relationship.

Few journeys have more frequent ups and downs than those experienced by gamblers. Their gaming experience involves a "tidal wave of emotions" that accompanies winning and losing. When asked to describe their gaming experience, all gamblers in a study about the casino experience framed it as a journey with ups and downs. Gamblers pointed to financial ups and downs and emotional ups and downs. As you may have guessed, the financial and emotional metaphors were very closely tied. Conventional wisdom suggests that die-hard gamblers would much prefer to arrive at a casino and strike it rich on their first hand of blackjack or their first pull of a slot machine. Who would not? But most serious gamblers prefer journeys with some downs. That is, the feeling of losing money—and the accompanying frustration and anxiety—factors into their experience as long as they end up winning more. For gamblers, there is emotional reward in experiencing the ups *and* downs.

Fast and Slow Journeys

The gambling journey takes place at a "high speed," especially in the up moments. Another type of high-speed journey frequently mentioned by consumers in a variety of studies is the pace of today's rushed society. Individuals often feel as though they are in a race to get things accomplished or are being chased by some antagonistic entity. Time is "slipping through their hands," and they have a hard time "keeping up," never quite "catching up," while "deadlines are looming" everywhere. The emotions typically felt in such instances are stress, anxiety, and lack of control. Travelers use massage services in airports as a brief relief station to cope with these experiences while on literal journeys. On the other hand, a fast journey, when successful, can lead to feelings of accomplishment. Distance learning programs and other programs designed to teach foreign languages or computer skills quickly are good examples. These programs build on the emotional satisfaction as well as the practical benefits of a fast-track solution.

Depending on the context, slow journeys, too, can have positive and negative connotations, depending on the context. A positive slow journey allows actions to be unhurried and relaxed. The result can be a reduction in stress, rejuvenation, or a new perspective. In one beverage study, a consumer described in the vignette step of her interview a fantasy scene in which she and her boyfriend are at a tropical beach, rip up their airline tickets, bury them in the sand, kick off their shoes, toss aside their luggage, and pass one another a bottled beer. Here, the journey home was slowed to the point of termination. On the other hand, a negative slow journey takes place at a sluggish pace and produces frustration and feelings of lost efficiency. Two symbols commonly used to describe a negative slow journey are snails and turtles. Long lines at a checkout counter, rush-hour traffic, and poorly developed movie scripts are all examples of journeys that move at a "snail's pace." Pfizer print and TV ads feature a hare and tortoise, building on their fabled race, won by the persistent tortoise, to promote their smoking-cessation medication, Chantix. One of the journey-oriented tag lines used is, "On the quitting road, it's all about getting there."

Summary

Journey is one of the most widely examined and universally felt deep metaphors and appears as a major theme in literature around the world. Journey is rooted in our awareness of time, evolution, progress, and maturation. The consumer often experiences himself or herself as on a journey and sometimes experiences others on a journey. Even objects or events are journeys, which may come at us quickly or slowly.

- Journeys may have known or unknown outcomes.

- Journeys may be smooth or may involve many obstacles, and most journeys have their ups and downs.

- We take journeys alone, with others, for our own benefit or the benefit of others.

- Because these journeys serve as the backdrop to people's life stories, our interactions with consumers can prove more successful when we take the time to focus on the themes that a particular journey holds.

6

Container

How Inclusion, Exclusion, and Other Boundaries
Affect Consumer Thinking

The container deep metaphor involves physical, psychological, and social states and sometimes a combination of all three. Containers perform two basic functions: they keep things in and keep things out and they are pervasive. Gated residential communities and border fences form clearly defined physical barriers intended to provide a sense of security or, as some remember for the Berlin Wall, of imprisonment. The old phrase "You are what you eat" is a caution that what enters your body (among our earliest associations with container) defines both its status and even that of another powerful container, one's self-identity.

Similarly, theatrical productions occur within physical locations and contain emotional experiences by drawing in audiences with captivating performances. The American League of

Broadway Theater Owners and Producers wanted to increase attendance at Broadway shows. The league first studied theatergoers to understand their thoughts and feelings about the role of Broadway theater in their lives. As it turns out, theatergoers described the experience of immersion in a play as an escape from their overcrowded daily lives. Attending a theatrical event "opened a door" to another world and left daily obligations and pressures behind. One person stated, "I am in this little theater and the whole world is outside, but I do not notice it. The theatre is a sanctuary. Everyone's cell phone is off. There are no beepers." (Figure I-5 in color insert.) This notion of escape refers to the deep metaphor of container. The league is leveraging these powerful container themes—escape *from* worries and *into* somewhere else—in its communications materials.

A *container* is a physical, psychological, or social "place." We are "surrounded" by container metaphors, which are often revealed by figurative uses of the words *in* and *out*.[1] We might feel "left out of a conversation" or we can get "into her good graces," even though neither a conversation nor someone's goodwill is a literal place. We say, "Keep your nose out of other people's business" to indicate an inappropriate or uninvited invasion of someone's personal space or affairs. We find ourselves in a good mood, in good health, a member of the in crowd, or perhaps feeling like an outcast. Optimism and pessimism are represented by describing our glasses as half-full or half-empty, and if we are overloaded with responsibility we say we have a full plate. Our computers have "Intel Inside." Taco Bell asked us to "Think outside the bun." Managers are encouraged to "think outside the box" when they are bound by routine thinking. Thinking outside the box means moving from one's customary "box" and into a novel "box."

Consumers often view life itself as a container: "She leads a full life," "My life is empty," and "Life is full of surprises." Marketers speak of consumer needs to fill and describe how goods and services can put meaning into their lives. The very concept of self is like a Russian doll, a container with different selves nested within other selves—an "onion peel" theory of personhood, wherein our outermost layers are public and our innermost layers are private and potentially unknown and unknowable.[2] Outer layers can mislead—"Beauty is skin-deep"—or show only part of who we really are, and so we acknowledge other selves within us. For instance, "That manager seems like a jerk on the surface, but he really is a nice guy at heart." Language itself is a container; sometimes putting our thoughts *into* words is easy and other times getting our thoughts *out* is difficult.

From Womb to Tomb: The Origins of Container As a Deep Metaphor

Container metaphors are fundamental because human beings are themselves containers of bones, blood, and brain that travel from one container (the womb) to another (the tomb).[3] We learn early in life that our bodies are semipermeable containers keeping gas, liquids, and solids in and out. Eyelashes keep dirt from our eyes; pupils let light in. Tears flow from ducts; blood clots in cut skin. Our digestive and cardiorespiratory systems maintain an equilibrium between what comes in and what goes out. So basic are these bodily functions to our well-being that when our bodies fail as containers, our lives are turned upside-down, physically, emotionally, and socially.

Research indicates that our existence inside the womb stays with us. In its later months of development, a fetus can hear sounds from outside that first container. French physician Alfred Tomatis has found that children who exhibit difficulties listening or speaking can show dramatic improvement in those areas after hearing recordings of their mothers' voices played back through a filter designed to replicate how her voice sounded in utero.[4]

Like all deep metaphors, container stems from sensory and motor systems and their interactions with our social and physical environment.[5] Since all human beings rely on these systems and address the same basic challenges in their environments, consumers around the globe use very similar container metaphors.[6] For example, comparing anger to a hot fluid in a container appears in many cultures, giving this intangible emotion a physiological base.[7] In the United Kingdom and the United States, one hears statements like "The customer is just blowing off steam," "He was about to blow his top," and "Those call-center attendants make my blood boil." In Hungary, one might hear "Anger was boiling inside him," and "She was all steam." In Japan: "My anger kept building up inside me," and "The shopper got all steamed up." In China: "One's qi wells up like a mountain" (qi is the life force within the human body). In Zulu South Africa: "When I told him, he inflated," and "She was so angry, she burst." In Poland: "He is boiling with rage," and "She burst with anger." In Tahiti: "The angry man is like a bottle. When he gets filled up, he will begin to spill over." In Germany: "She is foaming over with rage."

This chapter looks at some of the many instances in which this deep metaphor affects consumers' thinking and behavior. Examples range from how we view our memories to how we feel about clean clothes.

Figure I-1: "Coming Full Circle" as a New Mother

Twenty-year-old "Jenny" used the language of container, journey, and balance in explaining her digital image about becoming a first-time mother:

> "The strand of pearls connotes the circle of life. Within that circle, a budding, pinkish red flower supported by a vase represents a new baby girl and the shape of her life. The other transparent flowers, fading into the bottom of the vase, represent all the phases she has already gone through, memories of my first year with her. Just to the right and touching the flower is a female elephant that represents people like my mother-in-law, who spends a great deal of time with my daughter. She steps into and out of the circle at different times. She actually has some colorful paint on her, as she is always fun for my daughter to see.
>
> "Above my daughter is a diamond—her birthstone—representing the purity, brilliance, and clarity of our new baby. It hovers above her because it also represents the life, happiness, and learning I want for her.
>
> "In front and to the left, but also inside the necklace are a clock and a juggler—more about me than about my daughter. There never seems to be enough time, whether I am preparing for my new baby or enjoying every little aspect of her life while having my own life. I constantly juggle when to stay home with her and when to leave her with someone while I clean house, go to work, or go to the store. The clock also represents her schedule, not something she controls but something I must know and respond to. The juggler's balls of many colors show everything I juggle in my day. Having a baby is a balancing act—not bad, but busy.
>
> "Completely outside the necklace is a bathtub, an escape for me. As much as I love my daughter, I sometimes must get away by myself or with a friend. In the middle of the image is the color red, coming from the necklace and maybe even the source of the flower's color, because it is how much I love my daughter in my life and how thrilled I am to be her mother."

Figure I-2: "Balanced Harmony" of Top-Shelf Vodka

A consumer of vodka expressed the deep metaphor of balance in the taste of a certain brand of vodka, specifically the alignment of nature—the freshness and quality of ingredients—and nurture—the handcrafted distilling process:

> "The tree with the potatoes hanging from its branches represents the importance of the freshest, best ingredients. That is why I colored the potatoes gold with sparkles coming from some. But, even with the best ingredients, you need skill to blend all those ingredients, like the grace of the experienced ballerina under the tree. I could have put a master furniture maker there instead. Everything must come together perfectly. When the ingredients and the human care harmonize, you get an authentic and original vodka, a true performance, a genuine piece of furniture. The work desk on the seesaw means that I put my best effort into my job, and I am that person relaxing on the other side. You can feel the vodka restore your calm. It is a true vodka, not a pretender."

Figure I-3: The Transformation Corridor in a Hospital

In hospitals, transformation involves both the physical and the emotional. Patients, their parents, the hospital staff, and visitors all express being emotionally transformed by their hospital experience. Architects translated this deep metaphor into design elements of the hospital's interior. For example, they used butterflies, an archetypical expression of transformation, in this corridor to create an immediate sense of transformation for everyone entering the hospital.

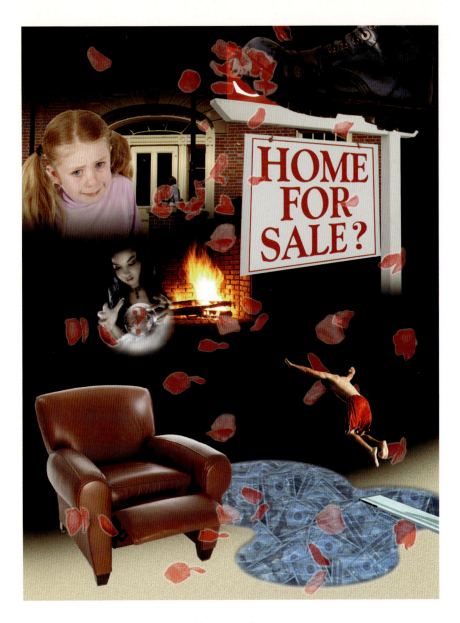

Figure I-4: "For Sale" Signs of an Unknown Journey

A young Minneapolis married couple jointly created this image about buying their first home, a frightening journey for the wife:

> "When my father lost his job, we had to sell our house and leave the neighborhood. That is what the 'For Sale' sign means to me, and I am that crying kid in front of the school. I remember how sad I was to leave my friends and my school. Those signs always scare me now and make me wonder why those houses are for sale. I wonder, 'Does that lie ahead for us?' My husband has a really good job and I cannot imagine our both not working. But I am not the fortune-teller confidently peering into the crystal ball in the picture. She probably sees a nice, big, positive exclamation point. Me? I see that big red question mark. The boot on that man's foot means that I would rather be kicked out of an apartment because we could not pay the rent than lose a house because we could not make the mortgage payment."

Figure I-5: The Broadway Theater Experience as a Container

Using enveloping language that revealed the deep metaphor of container, one theatergoer explained his experience of the theater:

> "The man floating means that the emotion onstage sweeps you up. You may get swept up in costumes, makeup, and the sets, or you get really sucked up into the story itself. You forget about everyday aspects of life and just enjoy being at this play. The circles in yellow represent that floating, being-swept-away feeling in the whole experience."

Figure I-6: "Cisco Systems, the Connection to the Source"

One customer expressed how the company-customer bond, rooted in an emotionally significant bond, enhanced the customer's feelings of connection with the world:

> "The world as the background shows how Cisco Systems can connect the whole world, every location, remote locations, homes, companies, offices. It connects one side of the earth to the other side. It seems hopeful and optimistic; it gives reasons to connect. It is not a real bridge, an obsolete object that you walk on. It is a rainbow that seems more like the future, more of a wireless gas. The little girl is holding the future. That is vital. It is life. She is connecting the world that she is holding, the world that she received, to the world that will emerge from people in the future."

Figure I-7: The University as a Resource for Life

One consumer described her expectations of her alma mater, explaining that the university should be a resource throughout her life, providing not only support and guidance but also joy and energy:

> "The stand of trees with a path through it indicates that the university is a constant in my life. The clocks around it are my past, my present, and my future. The other images symbolize what I expect the university to provide to me—the diamond ring means stability and the crossword puzzle means the ability to teach people how to solve problems and be an asset to the community. The fireworks signify this energizing, happy, good feeling that I have when communicating with the university because I had a positive experience there. The younger girl, who looks contented, is looking up at me. She looks up toward the high-rises going toward the light and feels a connection toward the future and possibilities. In essence, my relationship with the university gave me possibilities in my life."

Figure I-8: How Morning Rituals Affect One's Control Over One's Day

A 34-year-old single woman explained how her experiences in the morning affect her sense of control for the rest of the day:

"If my day starts well, it could be because I took allergy medicine the night before. I can start the day without my allergies running my life. I am often tied up in traffic; there are many accidents on the highway to work. Those events are beyond my control but still stress me out and make me late. So the car on the road means no traffic. I would love to drink a magic potion that makes me feel as good and in charge as when I woke up. Superwoman's drink. On the table, a pitcher of orange juice next to an orange tree means health. It would always be there, every day. If you feel good, then you have a positive attitude. That attitude spreads to people you encounter, and so you can accomplish more. Music is another great start to my day. Musical notes are all over because the right kind of music in the morning can really uplift your spirits and give you positive images and thoughts. Then I would feel in charge."

The Mind As Container

Although the most obvious examples of the container metaphor evoke physical objects, the mind is the most common container. Knowledge, memories, and emotions—our entire sense of self— are the precious elements contained within the mind. The mind represents a unique container that each person considers his or her own, inviolable space.

Memories

We often regard our memories as our most personal possessions. They contain who we are, our defining personal and cultural stories.[8] Not coincidentally, the words *storage*, *store*, and *story* have a common derivative involving container. Moreover, memories are malleable and dynamic, not fixed containers.[9] Although digitized photographs, video, and audio can preserve records of our unique personal moments—"Is it live or is it Memorex?"—and Web logs can capture our innermost thoughts and feelings, computer hardware increasingly stores our more factual, transactional memory in documents, software code, Internet pages, and databases, whether we want it to or not. When hackers steal—or when companies exploit or mishandle—that memory, especially without our knowledge or permission, we feel violated or invaded.

The memory container performs many functions for consumers. For example, a major hotel and resort chain wanted to understand what "get away" meant to consumers. It discovered that memories have restorative qualities; they help consumers replenish themselves. One consumer explained, "When I go on holiday, I sit at the beach or on the balcony and say, 'How beautiful this moment is.' My mind can store that feeling for a very long time. When I am at work, the image of that beautiful day pops up and makes me feel much better." Subsequently, the chain developed a special set of communications that it delivers periodically to remind previous clients of peaceful settings and their experiences at the hotel or resort or nearby locations. The captions of the images in these communications stress the special feelings that these places evoke, once someone has experienced them.

In a study of the tagline "feel good," we found that memory holds feelings of pride and experiences to share with others: "Having memories is important. I revel in the past. I do not want to forget what makes me happy or proud. I want to keep and share those positive feelings." Notice how this consumer refers to memories as something to have, keep, and share, as if she can possess memory as a container. Indeed, memories enable us to hold on to time and even slow it down. The metaphor "hold on tightly" occurs in this customer's comment on the use of imaging software for computers: "I always feel that time is passing too quickly and running away from me. There are certain situations where you are happy, lucky, lusting for life, and you want to capture and hold on tightly to them. Whenever you feel bad, you can look at these pictures again."

In a project for Hallmark Cards, Inc. on the meaning of memories in people's lives, we found that consumers thought of their memories as containers: "A person's life is like an hourglass. The grains of sand inside are the memories that constitute that life and everything that happened to it. The sands start falling when you are born. At first, there are few memories.

Sand falls throughout life so that, when all the grains reach the bottom, you could have seventy or eighty years full of memories."

Feelings

Sometimes, we are devoid of feelings or overflowing with them. A variety of goods and services ranging from prescription medications to self-help books and help-lines promise to release difficult feelings. Consumers perceive many beverages as providing this release: drinking tea, warm milk, hot chocolate, and alcohol. In a study for a major beer company, consumers described their daily lives as filling them with worry, stress, and self-consciousness and felt occupied by events producing these feelings. Thus, consumers felt "full" of unpleasant qualities. Having a beer at the end of the day, however, alters the contents of one's thoughts, filling consumers with such "good stuff" as energy, peace, comfort, a reward, time, and a healthy perspective. "The bad stuff that daily life puts in you gets drained out when the beer goes in," said one consumer. The theme of beer's draining away the negative and pouring in the positive was powerful. The company built on this theme in its communications showing beer pouring with gusto into a glass, which consumers saw as a container symbol of their bodies.

The Body Is a Fragile Vessel

In a pharmaceutical study of sufferers with recurring bouts of diarrhea, container metaphors structured these consumers' thoughts about the physical discomfort, lack of control, and shame associated with chronic diarrhea. When the first symptoms of diarrhea struck, patients felt as though they were about to lose physical control; their bodily containers were quite literally about to burst open: "I feel like I am a volcano ready to erupt." "Diarrhea just drains you. You just want to lie there because it just zaps your energy and takes a lot out of you." Consumers viewed solutions in container terms: "I picture the medication as a lid on Tupperware to contain the problem and calm me down." "I picture the medication as a superhero who can build a wall to stop the flow, to create some net or wall to contain it."

In a study for a leading brand of toothpaste, we discovered how people view bad breath as a social trap and toothpaste as a means of escape. In general, they view personal hygiene products as enablers for entering into social relationships, which are also containers. One person described how toothpaste liberates him from fears of bad breath: "When I do not have fresh breath, I cannot speak freely. I fear someone's smelling my breath. After I brush my teeth, I no longer worry. I can have fun, be more intimate with someone, as if I were sprung from a trap."

Like many respondents, this consumer viewed his mouth as a container of breath that frees or constricts social interactions, and toothpaste as a resource for altering—cleaning—the inside of this container. Using the right toothpaste freed consumers socially because it removed bad breath. One of several uses of this insight involved the redesign of its packaging to contain cues that consumers understood as liberating.

Culture As Container

One of the largest containers is culture. People enter or leave particular cultures that are containers of various subcontainers of shared beliefs, values, customs, objects, behaviors, and the institutions that give rise to them. In a study of second-generation Hispanics in the United States, participants spoke of the challenge of living in two containers (two cultures): "My father came to America when he was eight years old, and forgot his past. He threw it away. He did not want to be seen as an outsider, and so he Americanized himself. I did not learn Spanish, because he never really spoke it in front of me. He regrets losing it and he regrets not teaching it. I would love to learn Spanish. It opens so many doors for people." Notice how the speaker's father wants to be *in*side and not *out*side the container of American culture. The speaker wishes he could speak Spanish because the language "opens so many doors for people," presumably doors that open into new containers. Of course, the very container that his first-generation father "threw away," the second-generation speaker now wishes had been kept.

Minority groups face discrimination in various sectors of American life. In the digital image in figure 6-1, a second-generation Hispanic American described her experience; her exclusionary language also revealed the container metaphor at work.

Even though "Latinos are making it up in the world," and have entered the container of American cultural success, Latinos still feel "fenced in" by cultural discrimination. A leading human resource consulting firm has integrated this and other insights from the research into the instructional programs for its clients.

Places As Containers

We noted earlier that physical settings as containers can affect social and psychological experiences that "contain" values, beliefs, and emotions.[10] Experience Engineering is a pioneering firm that uses customer experience clues to shape a more desired

Figure 6-1: Culture As a Container That Includes or Excludes You

"I used the barbed-wire fence as a background to symbolize the struggles or barriers that we Latinos have to cross every day—in our workplace, in our school, or in our personal life. In the back, the building with many heads means that, even though many of us Latinos are moving up in the world, we still have many barriers to cross."

consumer experience for its clients. Experience Engineering worked with one of its clients, Northcentral Technical College (NTC) in Wausau, Wisconsin, to design a better experience for students.[11] For example, NTC is planning to add to its Health Science Center a four-story atrium that metaphorically cues students to the expanded horizons in store for them. Additionally, the college will design public meeting spaces, both inside and outside the classroom, to enhance collaboration, thus ensuring that people feel as if they are in the "same place" (or container) together.

Workplace

The container metaphor is commonly evoked when people think of escaping their workplace. A quote from a study for a major beer company illustrates escaping from a workplace state of mind and entering another state of mind: "When you hit the time clock on Friday, you think, 'I am done. I have until Monday morning; now I am free.' I do not have to answer to anybody or be in a certain place at a certain time or leave at a certain time. Just freed up." The sentiment of the workplace as a prisonlike container dominated by superiors contrasts sharply with the freedom the consumer feels on being "released" on Friday. In this case, beer is outside the prison, a symbol of weekend freedom. Other consumers in this study viewed beer as a tool to help "break out" or get away from the responsibilities of everyday adult life. In fact, one of the most important decisions for any new building is window design. Specifically, architects focus on using windows not only to let light in, but also to "let people out." Glass creates a more open, permeable container, thus allowing people to feel a part of the larger "outside" container.

Hospitals

A hospital about to undergo major renovations wanted to understand how patients and staff experienced its current hospital environment. Patients described the existing hospital as functional, but unremarkable. It met the most basic needs of patients and staff, but the drab surroundings and tight spaces made for an experience that was physically, spiritually, and emotionally confining: "You feel like a dog in a cage. You cannot go to a better space if you want to. It is uninspiring. It is bare. It is like being on a long flight in an airplane. It is your only space."

Patients draw conclusions about the quality of care based on the environmental cues: "Chairs that might not match and curtains that are hanging down—if I go to a place like that, I will not be as confident about the care that I receive, because I would wonder why they are not keeping up with the state of the art."

Patients (like all people) tend to match their emotions to their surroundings. If patients feel contained in a comfortable, relaxed environment, they will likely feel better about themselves than if surrounded by chaos or indifference. Said one administrator about the effect of a soothing, well-designed office on patients: "Your behavior matches your surroundings. A lot of our patients came from prison. Our TV room is probably like the kind of TV room they had in prison. So they act out. But they like coming into my room. They say they could spend the rest of their life here because of its decor. As soon as they walk in, they breathe a big sigh of relief."

Even though hospital buildings and rooms are literal containers, a room decorated to be relaxing feels like "an escape from" rather than "an entrance to" a container. More accurately, the prisoner-patients are escaping a restrictive container and entering a relaxed container. A facility designed with "relaxing containers" hopes to provide this hospital with happier patients, which could result in higher patient-satisfaction scores and potentially quicker healing.

Sports Stadiums

Physical containers also hold cues for emotions and memories that might not be obvious at first.[12] For example, in the late 1990s, the owners of the Boston Red Sox announced their desire for a new stadium. Fenway Park, built in 1912, greatly needed improvement. But fan reaction was swift and unsupportive. Why? Because baseball stadiums are containers of collective as well as personal memory. They keep alive the history of the game and, more importantly, fans' personal histories. One Red Sox fan said, "I have more than a half century of sunk costs invested into Boston's hard luck, yet venerable, baseball team and its treasured home. A couple of years ago I took my 17 year old nephew to Boston with the premise that if I should suffer for half a century, he might as well catch the Red Sox-Fenway Park 'virus' and suffer too. For tens of millions of New Englanders, historic Fenway Park is their personal field of dreams."[13]

The love affair with Fenway Park has less to do with Fenway itself than with what is figuratively inside: memories of long-ago heroes and long-deceased family members and friends are somehow still alive and safe within the ballpark's walls. The Boston Red Sox sold the turf they replaced after winning the 2004 World Series. One promotional theme suggested placing this turf on the graves of deceased fans, and many turf buyers did just that.

Products As Containers

British postmodern novelist Angela Carter once said, "A book is simply the container of an idea—like a bottle; what is inside the book is what matters." For example, the *New York Times* contains "All the news that's fit to print." Of course, people do judge books by their covers, and external cues can affect how consumers experience a product's contents. But what is inside counts, too.

Beverages

The container metaphor fits aptly for many beverages, including soft drinks. A study for Coca-Cola in Germany, Greece, and the Netherlands illustrates several container themes. Coke was described as a container of positive emotions that flow into yet another container, the body: "If one is in a bad mood and drinks Coca-Cola, that makes you happy again and one even looks happier. Other people see that you are happy and then tend to speak to you. One is not so miserable and sad." This sentiment resonates with Coca-Cola's former tagline, "Have a Coke and smile."

In another case, the joy of Coke is so strong that it explodes from the body: "When I am just sitting there and my head is empty, then I think to myself, I will drink a sip of Coca-Cola and then I will feel better right away. I can concentrate much better on everything, and I also feel more refreshed. Everything just bubbles out of me when I get this new surge of energy." Thus a Coca-Cola bottle contains a soft drink, but it also contains excitement, energy, and good mood—"the pause that refreshes."

Personal Organizers

Containers perform organizing functions. In a study for a manufacturer of paper and electronic calendars, appointment books, and related products, consumers frequently noted that these devices contain their daily life. One person described her personal digital assistant: "It is kind of a purse for my daily life; it holds the keys to what my day is going to be like." In a study for America Online (AOL), the mother of a young child described the Internet as an organizing container that captures myriad information in one neat, accessible place: "I think the Internet opens so many doors to you that I am sure if my son learns how to work the computer, when he's four or five he can learn so many things. It is like you can have the encyclopedia right in front of you, you have different dictionaries in front of you."

Of course, the Internet or World Wide Web is not a physical net or web; we commonly talk about searching the Internet or going on the Web. In a study for a major Internet provider, one heavy user noted, "The Internet is becoming such a huge part of our lives, something that we take for granted—like a food staple, like rice. We are becoming so heavily entrenched in how it integrates into our lives." This person, like so many others in the study, sees herself as entrenched in the Internet even as it becomes entrenched in her life: she is contained while also being the vessel containing the experience.

Motorcycles

Freedom from a repressive or unpleasant container is achieved in many ways. A lone motorcycle on the open road is a uniquely American symbol for freedom, and a study about Harley-Davidson motorcycles brought up deep-seated metaphors for containment and freedom. Consumers described how the mundane repetition of life bored them and held them back from the excitement that they sought: "Work is like being held under water for a long time and then finally getting up for a breath of air" and "Trapped. I know I have to go to work every day and I have to do the same thing every day. It makes me feel cornered."

Many consumers in this study felt work not only constrained them but could actually harm them physically. Motorcycles epitomized the adventures that lay outside of the confines of work. Pre-ride, the consumers were restless: "When you're inside, there's only so many different things you can do. Then after a while, it's boring. You get cabin fever; you've got to get out." But once riders escaped the workplace (and sometimes their homes and families) they felt unrestrained: "The thrill of the motorcycle ride in itself, it's like taking me out of reality . . . Free from hold or restraint. It's like riding naked. You're not restricted."

The motorcycle dissolves restrictive containers, allowing consumers to express themselves freely. This consumer compares riding a motorcycle to the feeling of shedding his clothing; symbolically, he sheds the burdens of everyday life. All that remains is the true, uninhibited, naked self, mirrored and complemented by the motorcycle.

Clothing

Clothing, obviously, is a physical container that shelters the naked body. More deeply, though, clothing serves as a container of emotions, values, and basic personality. The act of purchasing and wearing clothes is not just a simple act of protecting oneself from the elements; it is an intimate and meaningful act of expressing the person inside the clothing.[14]

The same articles of clothing can express drastically different feelings. A uniform can cramp one person's style, while to another person, the same uniform can imply a sense of duty or affiliation. Clothing made for a special occasion contains predetermined social meaning: for example, a well-tailored business suit is a symbol of wealth, power, and competency. A white wedding dress symbolizes purity and femininity. Arriving for a job interview dressed in a T-shirt and sandals is frowned on because the wearer has framed him- or herself in the wrong way: the outside container does not show the same kind of professionalism that the applicant hopefully feels inside. Think about what putting on a costume means: the previous, everyday container is discarded, and a new container, perhaps one symbolizing mirth, silliness, and joking is entered. Clothing can transform the wearer with its self-contained meaning; it can even carefully construct a new persona.

At the store, mass-produced clothing on racks of hangers may be seen as an empty container into which a buyer's meaning, as well as body, is put. A study for a global retail giant found that once clothes are worn and familiar, they take on the wearer's characteristics: "They're personal items when they belong to members of my family, whom I have obviously warm feelings towards. So when I pick up their clothes and take them out of the dryer, they're nice and warm and I usually pick them up in a big ball. And it just makes me feel maternal because I think of my children and that their bodies are wearing those clothes. I feel close to them because I am holding close their personal things." This mother sees the clothes as a physical protector and embodiment of her children's bodies, as well as a container for her warm and maternal feelings.

Clothing can also be a stand-in for an absent person, or even a past stage of life. This is illustrated by a study on the meaning of clean clothes: "I just took all of my daughter's infant clothes. They were in a box, and I just laundered them all and got all the stains out, and it was such a feeling of like, wow, they're all brand new again, because they had been sitting in a box for six and a half years. It was like when she was little again. It makes me feel like I've preserved memories. It is how much I care about her stuff and, in other words, her." This statement reveals how much meaning a container can possess: when the mother washes the infant clothes, she is transported back to her daughter's childhood. The clothing preserves the memory of the complex emotions of raising a baby, even long after the baby has grown up. Thus physical objects become time capsules.

Using such insights, companies can train sales personnel in the type of imagery that will resonate with clients and the non-literal and literal language that is likely to bring such imagery to mind. The insights can also help marketers design product cues to activate those images.

Clean Clothes

The very act of making things clean can elicit strong feelings, as this next example shows. As if clothes were a second skin, washing clothes is compared to washing the body: "Your skin's hygiene and your clothes' hygiene—it is actually the same thing. The hygiene of the body and the hygiene of things on you go together. For me, it is the basics."

By washing clothes (which are metaphorical containers), one also washes, renews, or strengthens one's sense of self. Not washing clothes is frowned on, because it reflects poorly on the internal personality. Dirty, stained clothing evokes as strong negative feelings as clean clothing evokes positive feelings: "Washing clothes is the same feeling as running on the beach or working out—getting out the poison. In my daughter's school, there's a shelf where all the kids hang up their jackets. It is like you can smell the other kids' clothes on her coat, and that really bugs me—because other people don't take care of their clothes like I do."

This parent considers the child's clothing a container of maternal love: the condition of the clothes shows the dedication of the mother. Even the proximity of sullied coats intrudes into the safe container of a coat that the mother has prepared for her child. She wants the outer shell to echo the purity that she feels her child embodies. Biometric studies have confirmed that point-of-purchase cues for cleaning products can subtly but powerfully activate these associations.

Education As Container

Events such as entering college are also containers. We speak about being in school, entering academic programs, and getting out of school. In a study for the University of North Carolina at Chapel Hill, high-achieving high school seniors framed the college experience as an event that nurtures minds and personalities, one from which they will emerge a different and more mature person: "I feel like I am the little caterpillar now, and then I will go into college and I will come out as the person I will be for the rest of my life. It is just the final stage of maturing."

College is a metaphorical biosphere containing its own living, breathing "environment" in which students hope to immerse themselves in order to excel both socially and academically: "I am looking for somewhere that has an atmosphere of comfort, where all the students try to get along and work together."

Ideally, the college should not be a confining place. Students want to reach out into the "real world" while still retaining the sense of protection and relative safety of the college environment: "I want the university to be like a spider web. I want it to have connections and be reaching out into the community so you can get internships, community service through the school, and jobs."

These students wanted their university experience to resemble a balanced, semipermeable container. It should be alive and full of emotional and intellectual nutrients that allow the students to grow. At the same time, it should permit enough influence from the outside world so that the students are fully prepared to excel when they leave the university cocoon. In a sense, universities face the same challenges that parents face— how to keep children safe and protected without isolating them and putting them into a "bubble."

Summary

Although no pun is intended, containers are all-encompassing, ranging from cultural systems to particular thoughts and feelings that occupy our minds. Here are some examples:

- Consumers see themselves and many objects and events in their world as containers.

- Consumers' experience with a product or service is also a container, a story of good and bad thoughts and feelings, as well as filled and unfilled needs.

- Life itself is viewed as a container. This is one reason why storytelling is such an important way of understanding consumers.

- Our memories, feelings, bodies, and social and cultural environments are understood as containers, as are many products and services and the places where products and services are consumed or experienced.

Of course, not every product, feeling, life event, or memory that could be framed in the container metaphor is always viewed this way. A lot depends on the significance of a boundary that consumers do or do not want to cross. Managers need to understand whether a particular container state is one that consumers would like to enter or exit and whether products or services are perceived as facilitating those actions.

7

Connection

How the Need to Relate to Oneself and Others
Affects Consumer Thinking

H umans have a basic need for affiliation. This need played
a central role in the evolutionary development of basic
social units.[1] The need to relate to others and to oneself has also
established connection as a major and pervasive viewing lens
for all manner of issues, as we will see. It drives interest in Internet chat rooms, brand-oriented clubs such as Harley Owners
Group (H.O.G.), dating services, and a variety of so-called
badge brands.

Cisco Systems, a major supplier of networking equipment
and network management for the Internet, recently undertook a
major rebranding initiative because its managers felt that a true
emotional bond with its customers was missing. Cisco initiated
a study of key customer groups—business decision makers and

heads of information technology departments—to understand their perceptions of the brand. The company believed its customers viewed their relationship with Cisco in terms of a simple functional benefit without emotional significance.

Cisco was surprised to discover that the customers' bonds with the company were rooted in emotionally significant feelings of connection with the world. Regardless of their industry, job function, or technological expertise, Cisco customers credited the company with connecting them to the world. They described this connection as vital to fulfilling their professional responsibilities. The digital image in figure I-6 (in color insert) conveys one customer's rendering of the Cisco connection. The Cisco Systems brand team used the deep metaphor of connection to form the overarching positioning for its revamped brand image.

The Origins of Connection As a Deep Metaphor

Our sense of connection with—and sometimes isolation from—family, friends, coworkers, religious institutions, political parties, teams, and even ourselves emerged during evolution.[2] We are a social species and our brains are wired for social connection. Even seemingly individual qualities like emotions originate in social connections.[3] These connections are critical for survival. They also give meaning to daily life, and lie at the root of connection as a deep metaphor.[4]

In a famous experiment, psychologist Harry Harlow placed young rhesus monkeys with two surrogate mothers. The first group got a soft terrycloth "mother" that provided no food. The second group got a mesh-wire mother with an attached baby bottle of milk. By the end of the experiment, the young monkeys clearly clung to the terrycloth mother, whether or not it provided food, and chose the wire surrogate only when it provided food. Whenever researchers stuck a frightening stimulus into the cage, the monkeys ran to the cloth mother for protection and comfort; both these qualities of connection were more valuable than food.

Harlow's experiment demonstrates that comfort, attachment, and connection are essential needs and that tactile sensations factor into satisfying those needs. In *The Accidental Mind*, David Linden explains, "Our sensory systems appear to have some particular specialization for social interaction."[5] Seeing pictures of other people's hands or feet in painful situations activates in our own brain the regions that comprise the affective pain pathway. Our basic understanding of pain enables us to connect with another's pain through empathy. Even the "pain" of social exclusion from a favorite activity will activate the same neurological areas that record physical pain.[6] Being left out "hurts."

While academics often explore connection in interpersonal relationships, our need and capacity to form attachments involves more than other people and our inner selves. We form connections with a wide variety of things:

- Animals, as real estate maven Leona "Queen of Mean" Helmsley demonstrated by leaving her pet Maltese dog, "Trouble," an inheritance of $12 million and instructions that the pet be interred with her

- Objects, such as blues legend B. B. King's guitar, "Lucille"; or Charles Foster Kane's beloved sled, "Rosebud"; or TV character Carrie Bradshaw's Manolo Blahnik shoes or a lucky coin or rabbit's foot

- Places, such as our homes ("There's no place like home," said Dorothy in *The Wizard of Oz*), natural settings like Walden Pond, a neighborhood Starbucks Cafe, or a monument like the Taj Mahal

- Memories of events, such as weddings, birthdays, holidays, the Super Bowl, or the Olympics

Consumers develop strong ties with brands and the firms that provide them. We hear expressions like "comfort food" regarding macaroni and cheese and taglines such as "Nothing comes between me and my Calvins," by Calvin Klein Jeans, and "Like a good neighbor, State Farm is there," by State Farm Insurance.

The opposite of connection is disconnection, which Maytag Appliances leveraged first in 1967 in the tagline "Our repairmen are the loneliest guys in town." In a study of how people feel about business negotiations, executives used such phrases as "We were not on the same wavelength in our conversation," "We were miles apart in our thinking," and "They broke off discussion just as I thought we were reaching a common ground." Whether it is the presence or absence of connections and whether consumers view those states positively or negatively, the very idea of connection unconsciously shapes our judgments of the people, objects, places, and events that populate our lives.

Our bodies provide many symbolic bases for expressing connection or disconnection. Consider these expressions that advertisers have exploited:

- *She gave him a helping hand:* "You're in good hands with Allstate" (Allstate Insurance).

- *Reach out with all your heart:* "Reach out and touch someone" (AT&T).

- *It was love at first sight:* "The toughest job you'll ever love" (U.S. Peace Corps).

Our sense of physical orientation looms large in our expressions of connection: "He distanced himself from that position," "She felt very near to him," "They arrived at an agreement on that issue," and "I am stuck on Band-Aids 'cause Band-Aids stuck on me," by Johnson & Johnson for its Band-Aid brand.

Products That Bank on Social Connection

Given the major role social connections play in our lives, consumers naturally respond well when advertisers activate this deep metaphor. From beer to motorcycles to information technology, products and services that can capture the deep metaphor of social connection form a tight bond with consumers.

"Whassup" with Beverages?

Beverages are a product often consumed in a social context. We invite a friend out for coffee. We serve drinks to guests. Remember such catchy 1970s jingles as Lowenbrau beer's "Here's to good friends, tonight is kind of special," and Dr. Pepper's "I'm a pepper, he's a pepper, she's a pepper, wouldn't you like to be a pepper, too?"? We ritually offer a beverage to guests. We have tea parties. We have drinking buddies.

And we drink beer. In our study of emotion in advertising, sponsored by the Advertising Research Foundation (ARF), a Budweiser "True" commercial clearly activated the connection metaphor for consumers. The advertisement shows five twenty-something guys, each holding a bottle of Budweiser, enthusiastically screaming "Whassup!" into their respective telephones. Viewers tended to interpret "Whassup" as a social ritual involving friendship, the telephone, and beer. Indeed, the narrative implies that these fun-loving fellows are either establishing or renewing friendships. A telephone literally connects people, and inserting a Budweiser beer into the frame prompts viewers to associate beer with social connectivity.

Since the advertisement activated viewers' memories of similar rituals and social affiliations, consumers found deep personal meaning in this offbeat commercial. It resonated with their emotions. When asked for images to represent their individual memories of friendship and emotional connection, and to express the significance of friendship and connection in their lives, viewers brought pictures of children in a playground, adults playing touch football, mountain climbers supporting one another, and a school of fish.

Budweiser benefits enormously from the deep metaphor of connection. In referring to the "True" commercial, one respondent said, "The fact that all five guys in this commercial were drinking the same beer makes you wonder whether they became friends because they all liked this particular brand of beer." What's more, the Budweiser brand has long appealed to consumers by activating connection metaphors. When a brand succeeds in establishing a basic association (literally a neural pathway) in consumers' minds, subsequent activations of this association will continue to strengthen it. Eventually, an entire neural network, which associates Budweiser and connection, will develop in consumers' minds. As an added benefit, a brand that plants a metaphor deep enough to reorganize consumers' neural structures will prevent other brands from establishing this same association among consumers. In effect, the brand *owns* the deep metaphor—and Budweiser owns connection.

Social Membership and Environmental Belonging

Some brands are badges, showing that a consumer belongs to a valued user community. The Harley Owners Group (H.O.G.) proclaims on its Web site: "Express Yourself in the Company of Others. The Harley Owners Group is much more than a motorcycle organization. It's one million people around the world united by a common passion: making the Harley-Davidson dream a way of life."[7] This is a brand that offers emotional, physical, environmental, and even cultural connections for its owners. An American icon, it also connects consumers with their cultural roots and instills national pride. Harley-Davidson riders also develop connections with their bikes. Owners feel protective, much as a parent protects a child; H.O.G. members describe changing their bike's fluids as if they were changing diapers.

Newspapers As a Source of Connections

Before broadcast and electronic media became prominent, newspapers were king. Today, with new sources of textual content (e.g., the Internet and cell phone news alerts), the newspaper industry is fighting to retain its remaining crown jewels, not only through traditional printed news, but also through new media services. To better meet the needs of its readers, the *Pittsburgh Post-Gazette* studied the role of newspapers in readers' lives. As it turns out, the newspaper provides several powerful forms of connection, among other deep metaphors, to readers.

Newspapers enable consumers to connect with themselves. Through the paper's perspective on the news and editorials, readers question and reinforce their own beliefs and personal identity. They gain a sense of self by reading and asking, "How does this fit with what I believe to be true?" and "Will this news affect who I am as an individual?" Consumption of information educates readers, giving them more confidence in their life decisions: "I am a little wiser. More intelligent. More confident. This is my life, and this affects it. I want to know that my choices are the right ones for my kids."

The newspaper also fosters positive social interactions, such as bringing loved ones together. Spouses—and entire families—read it together and share it or its ideas with each other. The paper sparks family communication, which fosters bonding. One reader said, "Our little kid likes to sit with me and read the comics. The older one reads the comics himself but will call out, 'Mom, you have got to hear this one.' My husband and I discuss what we read in the paper that day and swap sections of it, and so it is a very big part of the family." Figure 7-1 depicts one reader's thoughts on how the newspaper connects and how he considers the newspaper a family member.

Viewing the newspaper as a way of connecting with others extends beyond the immediate family. With new knowledge, readers are more confident when participating in discussions with others—at the coffee shop, at dinner parties, at work, or in other social situations: "The paper informs people. You talk at work about what the current events are, give your perspective, your information, your knowledge, to another person."

The newspaper also connects readers to their community. By becoming aware of what is happening in their community, readers gain a sense of belonging: "We live here, and I like to

Figure 7-1: The Role of Newspapers in Connection

"The newspaper is another member of my family and central to our family experience. We share it together; it is part of our lives. The family is holding a picture of the globe, meaning that the newspaper brings the world home to me, makes it accessible to me, and helps me understand it. The cup of coffee indicates how reading the paper is as much a part of my daily and wake-up routines as my cup of coffee is. It is a ritual. The pack of vitamins means 'one a day,' my daily vitamin for my mind. The man with his face in his hands expresses terrible anguish; although I have very happy, wonderful feelings about newspapers, they also channel and provoke some very strong emotions, including terrible anguish over events in the world. To the right, the bunch of electronic equipment and trash can indicate my feeling that reading the newspaper is a nice break from the electronic noise of our world and our culture today."

know what is going on in the city. So, if we want to take advantage of events, we can do so, or we can use that information to plan our travels. We are connected." Interestingly, this connection to community ties back to self-connection. By having a sense of place, one can better understand oneself.

The newspaper connects readers not only to their immediate community, but also to society and the world. By reading about and understanding world events, consumers become sensitive to other cultures and feel less isolated: "The world is a lot smaller with newspapers. It brings the world closer together. We should understand each other as the world gets smaller because we are in contact with others a lot more." Having the ability to go online and conveniently share with a friend or colleague via e-mail an interesting article read in the hard copy of the paper is a way of further shrinking the world and letting others know you are thinking of them. Adding the relevant Web site information to the hard-copy version of an article facilitates consumers' connecting with others and expands the value of the newspaper.

Erectile Dysfunction As Disconnection

The deep metaphor of connection is very evident when consumers discuss thoughts and feelings about their health. Our health overtly and subtly affects our relationships with others; we all know instances in which illness brings people together or drives them apart. The frequently advertised prescription medications such as Viagra, Cialis, and Levitra for erectile dysfunction (ED) regularly invoke this metaphor.

Consumers viewed both the experience of ED and its solution in terms of the consumer's ability or failure to emotionally bond with a partner: "If you cannot have sex together, then you are just going through the motions of life. There is no excitement or connection between you." Interviewees feared their partners would seek fulfillment elsewhere: "Her T-shirt says, 'My boyfriend is out of town.' She is ready to try somebody else because her boyfriend cannot satisfy her." This dissatisfaction can lead to feelings of abandonment, loneliness, and isolation. One interviewee pictured himself on his own: "It is snowing out. I am cold because I cannot satisfy my partner. She is not happy, and so I cannot keep her. It is dark and dreary. With ED, I would be depressed and unable to start a family or have anyone to share my life with."

Even if the relationship does not fail, interviewees described a lasting tension in the relationship: "This slob on the couch represents another failed attempt where the outcome was inconclusive or was not particularly gratifying for either party. I am depressed and my wife is tense and frustrated. That tension carries into the week and makes the next attempt to connect sexually even more difficult."

A positive intimacy experience begets the anticipation of more: "When it has gone so well, there is more of a flow and a glow between us. We are both relaxed and get along better. The nice benefit is that it makes us more likely to want to do it again." Conversely, "If there is an opportunity to make love and we start but I cannot finish, the experience is frustrating and disappointing. We both end up feeling tenser because we know that it will be a long time before we make another attempt." Insights like these have been used to educate physicians about the many dimensions of ED among patients and to develop discussion guides to help physicians encourage their patients to discuss ED.

Be Careful How You Touch

Everyday conversation is rife with expressions that equate hands with the deep metaphor of connection. We say, "Lend me a hand," to ask for someone's help. Two people say, "Let's shake on it," when they've reached an agreement. "Taking someone's hand in marriage" connects us to a social institution as well as a highly personal commitment. Other expressions, such as "His hands are dirty," reflect a person who has violated social norms, while a person who is overcommitted by too many connections is said to have "her fingers in too many pies." The symbolic significance of hands is one reason why they are prominently cued

in advertising, logos, and product designs. Many ads have messages stressing the importance of social connection, which
hands help symbolize. The use of hands in advertising can distort our sense of product size. For example, when Apple first introduced its new iPhone, the official site displayed the gadget
being held in the palm of a hand. Later, a larger hand holding
the same iPhone in the same way was used to subtly convey the
impression of a smaller iPhone. This is a technique known as
forced perspective. Hands are so often present in advertising that a
hand-modeling specialty has developed for jewelry, clothing,
nail, and skin care.

One package-design study focused exclusively on the consumers' experience of holding different package designs for a
laundry detergent. Package designs that fit comfortably snug in
the hand evoked positive, caring feelings for homemakers, as
well as reassurance about the detergent inside the package.
These snug-fitting products were perceived as delivering
cleaner clothes and in providing "softness for my children. It
would make them think of me when they are at school."

A wide variety of products and services—such as nail salons,
jewelry, antibacterial hand soaps, hand creams, nail care products, and work gloves—are designed to benefit our hands. The
extent to which they satisfy our need for connection and pro-
pensity to view matters through that lens influences our assessment of their benefits and usefulness. In one consumer study on
hand care, consumers perceived hands as "a statement you
make about yourself," one that invites or discourages associations with other people. One consumer commented, "I judge
people by how their hands look, and I am sure they do the same
of me. I have seen some pretty creepy hands, and I am sure they

belong to a creepy person. I move away from them while I am on the subway, just because of their hands."

Hands create art, movies, clothing, books, houses, and so on. We still deliver important legal documents by hand, indicating the serious connection between the legal system and individual people. We value handmade crafts because of their connection to the jeweler, weaver, or potter. According to one consumer, bestowing handmade gifts is "like giving a part of myself to another."

Hands, of course, also make literal connections; they make direct contact between one's body and the surrounding world. We use our hands to touch, handle, finger, pat, and point. Hands can spread germs, and for many people hands bring germs to mind and invoke unwanted associations. In one company's study of how people view microbes in their environment, consumers saw hands as carriers of unwanted external substances into the body. One consumer said, "Humans are the transporters of what I do not want my hands to touch." Another commented, "No one knows where the things we handle come from or who else has been touching them. Some people can be filthy for a whole week, not bathing nor showering, and maybe they touch the same things you touch. That means you are in contact with them, too." Using these insights, the company reevaluated its messaging and discovered that it needed to soften the germ protection message. Because of the message, an already prominent concern had become even more salient and was thereby causing considerable discomfort among its customers. The revamped advertising resulted in a significant sales boost as consumers felt more comfortable at the point of purchase.

Owning Connections: Cisco and Penske

Budweiser seems to own the connection metaphor in the beer category, and Hallmark owns connection in the greeting-card category ("when you care enough to send the very best"). In the study of Cisco Systems described earlier in this chapter, the decision makers and information technology department heads we interviewed credited Cisco with building, even creating, the Internet, and with leading the networking equipment community, accomplishments synonymous with connectivity. One person commented, "I see the image of a spine because I feel that Cisco is the Internet's backbone. It holds everything together." Another noted, "Cisco is a bridge from where you are to somewhere else; it is a vital link. You can have a very formidable hardware, but you must communicate from one to another; communication, that bridging, is that link."

Conversely, the threat of disconnection led to feelings of isolation, anxiety, and even fear: "What would happen without Cisco Systems? There would be confusion, and nobody would know what to do and everybody would stumble. They could not communicate with one another. That would be very scary."

When a company or brand owns a deep metaphor, we often see the presence of conventional archetypes. The decision makers and information technology directors in this study referenced multiple archetypes. One was the father archetype: fathers provide connections for their children, helping to socialize them and prepare them for a life and career in a world with many other people. "I feel Cisco gives me a big boost, the sort you might get if you went into your dad's business." Others saw Cisco as the wise uncle: uncles are connected to nieces and nephews but not as closely as a father. "They are there when you need them but do not boss you around as if they always know better." In other in-stances, customers described Cisco as a big brother, more of an equal but with more experience in some areas.

Penske Truck Rentals owns various connection themes. A study with Experience Engineering revealed that the Penske brand invokes ideas of partner, team, and family. Some cus-tomers need a vehicle rental company that is like a business partner or even a true life partner: "I am going to someone who will work with me as I grow, and the person who works with me as I grow will be my partner. I do not treat Penske as a vendor. The Penske folks are partners because I need them. They want my business. Together we make that partnership work."

Some business customers feel the rental company is part of their team: "It is as if we are on the same team. We will get the job done, and the job is to get me out with a vehicle as quickly as possible. Like camaraderie. If there is a problem, they fix it."

Others saw an even closer connection with Penske, more of a close-knit family: "Penske is like family. A very supportive family. A very close-knit family. Not only with me, but with oth-ers. They know what is going on."

Another connection theme involved the special privileges and favored treatment of close connections. In some cases, con-sumers felt this treatment was guaranteed, as if by oath: "It is as if you go to the same restaurant all the time—you want the spe-cial table because you have your special girl with you and they can get it for you because you are in with them."

Health-Care Quality

The quality of health care concerns patient advocacy groups, var-ious health-care providers, and many other public and private

organizations ranging from governments to Web site information sources. The issue has many important dimensions, such as
facilities, treatments, the experience of a medical condition, and
so on. We have conducted many projects addressing health-
related issues and from multiple perspectives such as patients,
health-care providers and facilities, family members of the physically and mentally ill, informational Web sites, and pharmaceutical firms. Health-care quality often arises in these projects
even when that is not the study's primary focus. When questions of quality do arise among patients, one dimension domi-
nates all others as a viewing lens: the nature of the patient's
connection with the health-care provider.

For example, in one study, a person brought a picture of two
elephants with their trunks entwined and commented, "I like to
feel we are equal and that I am not treated as inferior. When a doctor treats me as an equal, I know he knows what he is doing; he is
not hiding behind a superior attitude or unclear technical stuff.
He respects my thoughts and we make decisions together." In a
different study, another consumer used a watch to convey the following thought: "I know I am in good hands when they sit down
and listen. That means they can help with everything, not just
with the first thing they hear. I am not reluctant to ask questions
about what I do not know." In a third study, a consumer used a
picture of a door to illustrate the difference between a physician
who gives good care and one who does not: "She will take time
and listen rather than have her hand on the doorknob, ready to
see the next patient. I would not trust what the latter doctor
would prescribe for me, because she really would not know me."

Some providers understand this sentiment. In a study of
health-care professionals, one commented, "Caring gives patients
a sense of security. It makes them more at ease. Sometimes, if

you just hold their hand, it does more than almost anything you could give them. They will have the faith to follow your advice fully." However, many health-care professionals place more weight on nonrelationship factors such as treatment efficacy, delivery issues, and facilities. Hence, when addressing health-care quality issues with patients or the larger consumer public, these professionals often stress factors beyond their audience's primary concern, which is connection.

Loyalty Is a Two-Way Street

Brand loyalty is perhaps the most discussed topic in marketing, and rightly so. The lifetime value of a customer can be very high and warrants the special costs of securing enduring commitments to your brand. Consider this consumer: "I am driving in the car, I am out of coffee, I see a Stop & Shop, and I say, 'Oh, I've got to get my coffee.' I go down the coffee aisle, and it is out of Taster's Choice. I must find another store that sells it. So I get back in the car, go to Star Market, go down the coffee aisle, and there it is, my Taster's Choice, and I say, 'See, I'm loyal to you. I purchased you. I will only buy you.'"

Consumers develop brand loyalty because the product consistently delivers what it promises *and* it resonates emotionally. However, just because the term *loyalty* implies a special connection does not mean a brand must activate connection as a deep metaphor to achieve consumer loyalty. Instead, the brand must effectively leverage any relevant deep metaphor to motivate product trial and the repeat purchase behavior that culminates in loyalty.

The Harvard Business School's Mind of the Market Lab conducted several projects for a consortium of firms owning some of the world's leading brands. The findings across projects emphasized loyalty as a reciprocal process. One business customer in the computer industry said, "I am giving loyalty and I am getting loyalty back. That is what loyalty is about, a two-way street. It feels safer for me when it is equal, when it goes both ways."

In our interviews with brand managers, we often notice that while they think of consumer loyalty to a brand, they do not think of a brand as loyal to its consumers. Consumers become aware of this one-sidedness. When asked, many loyal consumers did not feel that the company or the brand reciprocated their own commitment. While consumers may continue to use those brands and thus, by some standards, be deemed loyal, the loyalty is fragile. Consider these expressions:

- "I would not bank anywhere else. I opened my very first account here when I was younger, but frankly I do not think the bank really worries about my banking elsewhere. I am one of thousands. Why would it care about me in particular? My impression is that it does not."

- "They tell me in that chirpy, recorded voice that my call is very important to them and then they put me on hold forever, and I keep thinking, 'Like yeah, right, I am really important.'"

- "I keep going back to them because they provide a really high-quality product—because they worry about their competition, not because they care about me."

- "All these points programs. Or the coupons. I use them. But basically they are buying me; they are not being loyal to me. It kind of says, 'We must do these extra things because we are not doing enough with what we give you to begin with.'"

Many other consumer quotes suggest an asymmetry in loyalty. That is, the consumers feel more strongly connected to the brands than the brands are to them—not a healthy or secure foundation for building brand loyalty. Companies cannot simply offer quality products, because competitors can always emulate a quality product. Companies must convey that they have the consumer's best interest at heart. This is one reason consumers use their perceptions of how firms treat their employees as a proxy for how firms value their customers. As one consumer put it, "If they don't treat their staff well, you can hardly expect them to care about us."

Summary

We human beings have a fundamental drive or need for connection and, at times, for being disconnected. This has roots in our evolutionary history, because individuals and groups with the ability to bond and support one another were more likely to survive. Thus, the need for affiliation became an enduring driver of behavior. This need has extended to individual identity; in fact, it is said that the mind is not the possession of the individual and that our notions of self are determined significantly by the various individuals and groups with whom we connect. Sometimes, connection is expressed through the consumption of material things that reflect social membership, help us feel accepted, or demonstrate our relative position in society. Consumers develop strong attachments to objects, brands, and companies. Marketing managers must be sensitive to several connection-related issues:

- Connection is a two-way street, and consumers are more apt to feel loyalty to brands and companies if they feel those in charge have a commitment to them.

- Products and services can provide connection or disengagement, or both. The offerings may be a badge showing informal membership in a group or society (connection), may offer a means of being apart from others (status via disengagement), or may afford the consumer private time (disengagement).

- Other goods and services provide a sense of inner connection and a sense of connection with others.

Managers must identify the dimensions of connection that are most relevant or could be made more relevant to consumers. For example, managers need to consider whether a product offers connection with, or disconnection from, others or oneself. And they must decide whether a connection is physical, social, or mental. Once these levels of connection are understood, marketing managers can better show how a product or service attends to the consumer's basic human needs.

8

Resource

How Acquisitions and Their Consequences
Affect Consumer Thinking

Resources are capacities or abilities used to restore or achieve certain states. Because resources are so central to survival and feelings of satisfaction, we often use the concept of resource as a viewing lens for judging objects, people, and events. A resource may be physical (such as a tool, person, or organization) or intangible (such as a skill or body of knowledge). Resources act as agents enabling us to achieve important goals. In the strongest business relationships, both parties feel rewarded. American Insurance Administrators (AIA), a provider of insurance-related financial services to members of university alumni associations, wanted to understand the relationship between alumni and their alma maters to craft products more suitable for alumni and communications more personally relevant to them. According to the AIA's research, alumni framed their relations as resources for life. For alumni, if the school serves as a valuable resource after graduation, then it maintains a strong alumni relationship. Alumni expected their "return on investment" to exceed a college degree. One participant prepared a collage to explain what she expected after graduation (figure I-7 in color insert).

Even though alumni view tuition as an educational "contract" for a lifetime of support, universities view tuition as a four-year means to a terminal degree. This attitude often led universities to offer the AIA's products as new contracts with alumni. After learning about alumni's expectations, the AIA and its university partners began using language that establishes the original contract as still in place. For example, they used phrases such as "This new service is our way of continuing to give back to you," and "of making good on our end of the deal." After the implementation of this approach, response rates to AIA offerings improved considerably.

The deep metaphor of resource relates to capacities or abilities that we use to restore or achieve certain states. Since we rely on resources to survive and feel general satisfaction, we often use our understanding of resource to evaluate objects, people, and events. A resource may be physical such as a tool, a person, or an organization, or it may be intangible such as a skill, a body of knowledge, or a network of relationships. This chapter explores how consumers use the basic viewing lens of resource.

The Origins of Resource As a Deep Metaphor

The deep metaphor of resource involves the basic viewing lens of enablement and obtaining or retaining what we desire. Survival kits of rope, tarps, waterproof matches, bandages, iodine tablets, flashlights, and freeze-dried food remind us that our most basic human (indeed all creature) needs—water, food, and shelter—have remained unchanged since early hunter-gatherer societies.[1] Food and shelter are crucial to our survival.[2] We use resources to obtain other resources—for example, tools to acquire food, which provides another resource, energy. In a more general way, we view interactions with others as a resource that helps us obtain other resources. In a study for a leading retail chain store that examined sales staff morale, comments like "They are just using us up" and "We get chewed up and spit out" were common.

American psychologist Abraham Maslow famously proposed the theory of the hierarchy of needs. At the bottom of Maslow's hierarchy are our most fundamental, physiological needs such as food, water, air, and sex. Maslow believed that we must satisfy these basic human needs before we can move up the pyramid to "higher-order needs," which revolve around shelter and safety, and then on up to the highest needs, which include belonging and self-esteem. At the top is what Maslow called self-actualization, loosely defined as the ability to "be all that you can be" (as the U.S. Army first leveraged in its recruiting promotions in 1981). In reality, all these needs exist simultaneously, and one or more resources can satisfy them simultaneously. Do we need thirty-two flavors of ice cream, ten pairs of shoes, a bevy of medical specialists, a global positioning system on our dashboard, and a four-course meal at a five-star restaurant? Not really. But all these offerings do provide important gratification of some need.

Resource implies possession of an enabler; you either have or don't have enough. Furthermore, you can stockpile, deplete, or maintain a resource.

Consumers innately acquire, whether the acquisitions are necessities or niceties. Some sociologists consider the need to acquire—or accumulate resources—one of the most essential human needs.[3] To study how resources influence our lives, economists measure the supply and demand, production, distribution, and consumption of these resources. Money is perhaps the ultimate tangible resource for many people. The wealthy are "haves," and the poor, "have-nots." When we say, "Do not sell yourself short," we use fundamental economic principles to communicate that a person's resources—tangible or intangible—have value. "Time is money," Benjamin Franklin said, coining a motto for the American work ethic. We can save, waste, spend, and invest time. Miller Brewing Company utilized the resource metaphor in its well-known 1980s campaign, "If you've got the time, we've got the beer." In today's world of multitasking, time as a resource has become even more precious.

Applications of Resource

Broadly speaking, all products and services are resources enabling consumers to satisfy needs. For example, a bottled beverage quenches thirst, a help desk provides assistance, a financial adviser clarifies investment objectives, and an air purifier rids the air of toxins. Products and services often solve a basic human need and, in the process, provide higher-order social and psychological benefits as well. For example, a beverage may quench our thirst and give us a feeling of belonging to a larger social group. An air purifier may make us feel safer about our immediate environment and satisfied as a good parent providing a health setting for our children. The deep metaphor of resource so pervades our lives and language that we typically overlook its presence in our thinking and behavior. In fact, through resource metaphors, we can understand and experience most of what we want or need, under- or overvalue, and use to enhance our lives. Consider these memorable taglines for products and services, all invoking resource:

- "The ultimate driving machine" (1975, BMW)

- "The quicker picker-upper" (1991, Bounty paper towels)

- "Pardon me, do you have any Grey Poupon?" (1980, Grey Poupon mustard)

- "Put a tiger in your tank" (1964, Esso, which became Exxon)

- "You can trust your car to the men who wear the star" (1940s, Texaco)

- "Ace is the place with the helpful hardware man" (1970s, Ace Hardware)

- "Solutions for a small planet" (mid-1990s, IBM)

- "Leave the driving to us" (1950s, Greyhound)

The following pages introduce different forms of the resource metaphor, ranging from goods and services and the companies that provide them to our environment. Let us begin briefly with information and knowledge as a resource.

"The Mind Is a Terrible Thing to Waste"

The United Negro College Fund first used the notion of the mind as a resource in a campaign in 1972. In 1987, the Partnership for a Drug-Free America memorably used the theme: "This is your brain [image of egg]. This is your brain on drugs [image of egg in frying pan]. Any questions?"

Our mind—our intellect, cleverness, curiosity, ingenuity, and resourcefulness, all combining to address consumer needs—is an impressive resource. Successful people such as Oprah Winfrey and Martha Stewart "use their creativity," "use their smarts," and are "resourceful" or "endowed" with certain skills and talents, all of which are captured and marketed in their TV programs, magazines, and books. Consulting firms essentially sell ingenuity, creativity, and intellect bundled as expertise.

Knowledge, an understanding gained through experience and study, is perhaps the most prized resource, an observation widely documented in the fields of history and sociology of science.[4] Education, also a resource, allows us to study and acquire knowledge, and a substantial industry built around instruction exists to provide this resource. We talk about "knowledge capital," "knowledge base," "intellectual property," and "brain drains." Companies fight to acquire and retain talented individuals who have the knowledge to lead and make a difference in a given field. Citizens desire leaders who have the knowledge to govern wisely and well.

Information is also viewed as a crucial resource. We must master medical information if we are sick, financial information to plan for retirement, real estate information to negotiate shrewdly for a house, and political information to vote wisely.

Never before have we had access to so much information about so many topics, from air travel to zoom lenses. The highly successful For Dummies book series enables consumers to obtain information on just about any topic quickly and easily. The Internet, by far the greatest information source in today's society, has monumental potential for sharply reducing the gap between those who do and those who do not have access to information.

The Environment As a Resource

There are many who still remember the 1970s Keep America Beautiful public service announcement featuring Iron Eyes Cody as the "Crying Indian" who sheds a tear after a careless passenger in a speeding car throws trash that lands at his feet. Amid concerns of global warming and planet sustainability, the natural environment as a resource has become a powerful viewing lens that consumers use when thinking about various goods and services and the firms that offer them.

A consumer goods firm wanted to understand how consumers think and feel about environmental responsibility. The participants in the study invariably discussed the earth's importance as a natural resource. They spoke of proper and improper behavior regarding nature's wealth and the good deeds of saving and reusing natural resources as well as the recklessness of wasting them. Fear—the fear of running out of critical resources like water, air, and plant life in their or their children's lifetime—motivated their acting in an environmentally responsible manner.

The major barrier consumers faced in acting as responsibly as they should was the struggle to balance the consumption of other limited resources—time, money, and knowledge—with the consumption of natural resources. Many consumers described environmental responsibility as costly and time-consuming, because eco-friendly products were often more expensive and harder to find than conventional products. In addition, the consumers did not know how to learn which products were eco-friendly and which were not.

Consumers who already practiced environmentally responsible lifestyles expressed quite different opinions from those who said they did not have enough time, money, or knowledge. The environmentalists insisted that time and money could be saved by responsible behaviors such as riding public transportation and reusing materials. The frame of mind for this second group of consumers was that being responsible is an investment rather than a burden: "You reuse. That way, you need not produce more and it keeps costs down. Why buy the paper plates when you already have the plates? It is no big deal to wash. Not only do you save money, but you save trash and you save trees as well."

Eco-friendly products are viewed as resources for behaving responsibly. Such products allow consumers to wash dishes without harming the water, to protect the earth when growing vegetables, and to protect the air when cleaning the inside of their house. Consumers who are more responsible and accustomed to an environmentally friendly lifestyle were eager to encourage the general population to view eco-friendly products as valuable and attainable resources for protecting the earth from imminent destruction.

People As Resources

People are extremely valuable resources. Fortunate are those who can seek advice from a colleague, cry on a friend's shoulder, rely on a partner, or receive a get-well card from a neighbor. The elderly have invaluable experiences to share, the young have irrepressible energy, and those in midlife should have enough experience and energy to responsibly run the world.

Child development experts have found that socio-emotional support from family, friends, and community is essential for a child to survive and develop into a healthy adult.[5] Parents are arguably the most formative resource, providing children with guidance, nurturance, and protection:

- They help us grow into who we are.

- They shield us from harm.

- They support us in our decisions.

- They look out for our best interests.

- They save us from making bad choices.

Friends can provide similar resources. We even apply "worth" to our friends. We value friendship and count on close friends in times of need. And parents in turn need support from an extended family or a larger, like-minded community, or both.

In a consumer study, International Masters Publishers (IMP) explored what it means to be emotionally connected to someone or something and found the deep metaphor of resource prominent. Emotional connections, such as love and support, were resources that people found desirable to help advance and sustain the journey of life. One participant said, "Just as a really great parent can be an excellent resource to you, being emotionally connected to people or a group can benefit you through their knowledge." Consumers added that being open to others and building trust through meaningful connections was a necessary first requirement to exchanging resources with others on the journey.

Interestingly, resources don't just come in convenient, manageable packages. The resources available to us are complex, interconnected, and sometimes overwhelming. The consumer in the following quote felt stressed by a perception that she possessed unlimited resources of emotional support and empathy. She felt a responsibility to provide these resources, yet she also felt worried and burdened: "There are times when it gets a little overbearing. For example, my niece called me every day. I knew she needed emotional support, but it got a little wearing. I could not help taking on the burden."

IMP applied these insights to new-product development to reduce the complexity of maintaining connections in our lives. By integrating these findings into product design, IMP created a differentiated product in the market. Russ Ward, director of global research for IMP, explains that the company was able to develop a product that "provides improved emotional outcomes for the consumer, which can be directly communicated in marketing messaging—a huge benefit for the consumer and a win for IMP."

Psychologist Stephen Kosslyn explores social prosthetic systems. Kosslyn theorizes that just as a person missing a leg must be fitted with a prosthetic limb, we seek relationships with people who can balance our deficiencies. He uses the term "plug compatible" to describe how we extend ourselves through specific other people:

> More interesting, in my view, is that we rely on other people as extensions of ourselves. Specifically, we rely on other people to extend our cognitive and emotional capacities. Others help us formulate alternatives, evaluate options, and make decisions; others also help us interpret and control our emotions. Evolution has allowed our brains to be configured during development so that we are "plug compatible" with other humans, so that others can help us extend ourselves.[6]

Kosslyn also points out that when someone lends us his or her time and energy and the benefit of their expertise and experience, we extend our capacities by literally using part of the other person's brain.

Companies As Resources

In our business relationships, we find the same resource deep metaphor that we use in our personal relationships. Businesses look for partners who complement their strengths, help the firm grow, provide needed human capital, and so on. Within companies, there are human resource departments and professional development opportunities. Customers, too, look for relationships with companies that will extend their capacities, help them grow, and look out for their best interests. One consumer in a study on perceptions of big business stated, "This ladder reminded me of the best help desk I experienced for computer software. When I have problems with its programs, the company responds quickly, walking me through the problem step by step. I feel as if I am emerging from a deep hole as easily as if I were climbing that ladder."

Advertisements, done well, are viewed as another resource companies offer consumers, providing information about products or services and including guidance on the offering's use. A study by Condé Nast found that many consumers purchased single copies of special interest magazines primarily to consult ads relating to a pending purchase. The ads were viewed as major resources informing the purchase decision. One consumer in a pharmaceutical study on direct-to-consumer advertising viewed advertisements as a resource: "Drug ads give me more information about available drugs that I would otherwise not know about. If the drugs were not on TV or in magazines, I would never hear of them and they would not help me out. So drug ads are like protection blankets."

Ads can provide more than just information, though. Direct-to-consumer pharmaceutical ads can also be a source of hope and inspiration: "That ad says to me, 'Are you ready to believe?' You want to believe and you dream about the drug working for you. You want to believe that it will work, and so you are willing to try it."

Including hope in direct-to-consumer ads is a strategic decision, one meant to motivate the consumer to seek help from a physician. All advertisers go through a similar process of deciding what content or messages to include in their ads, on the assumption that the marketers are simultaneously deciding what content or message will fill consumers' minds. As we will see, however, in the cocreation of meaning, it does not work quite this simply in consumers' minds.

The Ritz-Carlton often uses resource as a deep metaphor in its communications. In one print advertisement, the hotel uses the image of a formal server's hand holding up a guest on a serving platter. The guest appears to be sitting down doing yoga or meditation with her arms outstretched. The imagery conveys to consumers that the Ritz-Carlton is a means (a resource) to help achieve emotional and physical rejuvenation. The server's hand—representing Ritz-Carlton's world-class service—is supporting the woman. The ad conveys a message that the hotel enables one to achieve balance in life, even if for a short time. It may only be for an evening, but the promise is that no other hotel will make guests feel so relaxed and calm.

The United Way logo also uses a supportive hand, a hand cupping an individual beneath a rainbow. Whereas Ritz-Carlton activates the theme of rejuvenation as a resource, United Way leverages the theme of community support as a resource. The rainbow image and the victory posture of the person held up by the hand communicate that the United Way is a helping organization. This logo also taps into the deep metaphor of balance. The person balances on the supporting hand in the same way that the United Way helps balance social and economic inequities. The United Way, therefore, is a resource for social balance. Again, two (or more) deep metaphors coexist as frames and reinforce each other.

Trust and Reciprocity

In a study for Harris Bank about consumers' relationships with their banks, we discovered that financial institutions are resources that consumers draw on for knowledge, tools, and other assistance: "In a financial institution, the knowledge is the experience that they have acquired over the years to provide whatever expertise is required to help manage my assets." As with personal relationships, the relationship between a consumer and his or her bank can cause anxiety if one party fears there is a resource inequality. For example, consumers risk their money, but they also risk the resources of time and energy in evaluating the bank and building a relationship with the bank: "It is a risk; it is a risky feeling, talking about your money. You work hard; you want to see it invested and capitalize on it like anybody else for selfish reasons. I always want more."

This risk is considered worthwhile if there is a reasonable expectation of a payoff in the end. Regardless, the consumer has invested a level of trust. Trust is perhaps one of the most valuable resources a company can share with its customers. One bank customer explained, "Trust is wonderful. It is what everybody searches for in this world in the products they buy, the relationships they have. It is what ties you to other people. Trust is very valuable."

Evolutionary psychology describes trust as a social lubricant.[7] Without a baseline level of trust, we would be armed with pointed spears, prepared to attack anyone in our immediate environment. Most people unconsciously follow a "gut" reaction, or instinct, when judging whether to trust or distrust someone. Trust allows us to conserve time and energy otherwise spent deciphering everything that we come in contact with and to instead reserve that energy for instances in which we should really be alarmed.

A project conducted by the Mind of the Market Lab at the Harvard Business School asked people across the globe the following question: "What is a company like that truly has consumers' best interest at heart, recognizing that companies have their own important interests, as well?" This question was asked of both consumers and managers. One major theme in the responses revolved around a company's ability to provide knowledge and support resources. One consumer said, "I would feel more confident knowing that someone out there is helping to lead and provide me with what I need to reach my goal. It may be just illuminating me about something. It is a feeling that I am not alone."

Another consumer appreciated a product that delivered what was promised and that therefore saved the consumer money, time, and the effort of looking elsewhere to find what she needed: "I am pretty happy because this purchase will do what it says it will do. I will not have to return it. I will not spend time tracking things down. It is a time-saving device. So I would say convenience and a time saver."

Archetypes: Hero and Protection

We touched on archetypes and their relationship to deep metaphors earlier. Archetypes often emerge from the deep metaphor of resource, as they are often enablers, that is, they provide something of value. For example:

- The "hero" provides protection.

- The "mother" provides nurturing.

- The "guide" provides direction.

- The "sage" provides wisdom.

- The "outlaw" provides a sense of rebellion.

Because archetypes are but one subtheme of a deep metaphor, they often convey only a partial picture to consumers about a company or brand. In fact, archetypes take on meaning only from the larger, more information-rich consumer stories in which they are embedded. For example, there is much more to a hero than his or her label. Heroes are often on a journey, a situation that requires understanding the type of journey. And, there is typically a goal in mind, perhaps providing liberation or freedom to others and thereby often restoring balance to a community.

Despite the limitations of archetypes, companies often take on archetypal roles, which help create the feeling that the company or its product is alive and is thus enabling a deeper connection with consumers.[8] In the aforementioned study for Penske Truck Rentals, the company's business customers ultimately viewed the company and its employees as guides throughout the rental process. One participant recalled the vulnerability that he felt without the company's help: "You are going into something where you have your eyes completely shut and then someone grabs your hand and leads you through the way."

The ideal rental company steered consumers through the process smoothly, making the overall move easier and less time-consuming: "Thank goodness for a soft touch. They handled me through the whole process with a soft touch. It was easy to make the reservation, easy to push up the time frame of when I was renting the truck, and easy to check out."

Having a trusted, reliable guide as a resource helped consumers feel in control on their journey. Listen to how the following consumer wanted to feel after a rental experience: "If you could go around all day, feeling as good as you do when you are curled up in your bed, then life would be pretty easy. Like at Penske, I just feel taken care of, secure, and safe. Worry-free. With little turbulence." Penske redesigned its consumer experience, from sales representative interactions to strategically selected artwork and visuals, to make sure that all its customers leave with this easy, curled-up-in-bed feeling.

In another global study for a major energy company, we asked commercial truck fleet owners and managers how they felt about motor oil. Resource surfaced once again as a deep metaphor that entailed many archetypes. Motor oil was perceived as:

- *An underappreciated hero:* "A policeman is never patted on the back for doing a good job. He only gets in trouble when he does a bad job. That is an accurate analogy for motor oil. You never think, 'Wow, is this oil great.' You think about it when it fails. Then, it is a villain, never a hero. But it is a hero to me."

- *A guardian angel:* "[Motor oil is] an angel just watching over, guarding, protecting all facets. I always think of angels as warriors, fighters. You never see them, but they are there, strong and multifaceted. We do not really see how they protect us. I never see my body fighting ten million enemies trying to attack. We have this product protecting and watching over us, unseen, doing what we never notice to keep us going."

- *Lifeblood for the truck:* "Blood does many jobs, if you think about it. It carries our oxygen. It carries our garbage. It carries the repair particles that fix holes in our system. It keeps us cool. Provides nutrients and a thousand other needs—all direct analogies with oil."

- *The root that nourishes a business:* "The oil can maintain the truck fleet like a stable tree. A deep-rooted tree, deep rooted to your business. If we have no failures in the engines, the business can go on and be prosperous and expand."

Each resource theme above connoted that motor oil and the engines it serves are "alive." These themes provided the energy company with several potential communications for positioning its product as the caretaker of the engine's life.

Food Products

Food is a resource that provides yet another resource, energy. The following phrases highlight the connection between food and energy.

- "I'm on a sugar rush."

- "I need an energy boost."

- "I felt drained after fasting."

- "She hasn't had her caffeine fix yet."

Manufacturers have designed many products to deliver such resources. For example:

- Gatorade as the thirst quencher

- Power Bar products as energy sources

- Double espressos as quick caffeine injections

In one study, we discovered that breath mints have multiple resource dimensions. First, they act as a personal cleanser. Some consumers even went as far as to describe breath mints as a detergent for the mouth: "It is like bleach. It makes your mouth feel nice and clean and fresh." Consumers described chewing breath mints as a protector or defender to "outsmart" their bodies and ward off cravings or as a substitute for eating: "If you crave eating something, you just put a mint in your mouth. Sort of tricking your appetite into thinking you are eating but you are not actually." Finally, breath mints act as a pacifier or calming mechanism for consumers, helping to release stress and tension: "It is like deep breathing or massaging your temples."

Resources for Health and Illness

Our bodies continually seek resources to help us reenergize, revitalize, or simply repair ourselves: air, water, food, rest, and so on. Serious health issues, on the other hand, require serious resources. When living with a serious disease or even a less serious ailment, consumers seek out resources such as physicians, family members, Internet sites, traditional medications, herbal remedies, and homeopathy. All these resources are enlisted with the goal of regaining control over one's health.

In a study about managing diabetes, various treatments were viewed as lifelong resources that patients could utilize throughout their battle with the disease. One consumer explained how she uses tangible resources such as medicine and medical equipment, but also intangible resources of love and support to accomplish her goal to "work at all this every day." In many health-care studies, patients cited similar resources to cure their ailment. However, because there is no cure for diabetes, resources can at best only be used to manage the disease. For the client sponsoring the study, this meant crafting its communications message to focus on medication as an important management tool, rather than something that will fix consumers. This focus made the company's communications more credible and trustworthy to consumers.

Perhaps the most important resource for patients, physicians appear as the hero or gatekeeper of all sources of power that the patient needs to fight the illness. Indeed, physicians view themselves through this same viewing lens. In a study about late-stage melanoma, one oncologist commented, "The patients look at the physician as a lifesaver and rescuer. It is no different for the cardiologist, it is no different with the pediatrician, and it is no different when our sons needed plastic surgery because of trauma."

However, when treating patients with advanced melanoma, physicians cannot be the hero or transfer resources, simply because by then treatment resources are severely limited. In a sense, the oncologist becomes an ineffective resource and often empathizes with patients as they, too, sense the losing battle with cancer.

In this scenario, hope may be the primary resource that a physician can offer. Physicians carefully use facts and statistics to provide hope to patients: "I must tell them that there is a chance that they will not be around in a couple of months, but there is a chance they will be around in three years. You tell them that they must hope for the best, but be ready for the worst."

Sadly, physicians often feel a sense of helplessness as their superhero powers dissipate and these professionals are relegated to the status of an observer. This was evident in an unrelated study of physicians dealing with a severe disease: "I have no tools, nothing to help them, to guide them on the way to make their journey easier. You feel very frustrated. You stand on the edge. You wish you could reach out. Unfortunately, we have nothing. If you do promise them hope, you walk into the quicksand yourself, because you are going to sink."

Then, too, there is a boom in wellness support systems viewed as preventative resources. One example provided earlier concerned the health ranch. A national fitness center found that its clients viewed their services as a "renewal home" and "the socket for my energy plug." A health maintenance organization conducted a study of the meaning of *well-being* and found that people viewed nutrition consultants, personal trainers, pets, and the clergy as "trustees of my well-being." These trustees were understood by many as essential resources for maintaining another vital resource, their well-being.

Summary

Resource as a deep metaphor is partly rooted in a basic need to acquire, as well as in our needs to achieve and maintain physical and social well-being. In a very broad sense, all goods and services are seen as resources to help achieve important conscious and unconscious goals. We often use the notion of resource as a way of viewing objects, people, relationships, and events in terms that transcend their immediate functional attributes. When a consumer calls an airline ticket agent "a lifesaver," we know that something much more important than a simple booking has been addressed. The deep metaphor of resource influences how consumers view accumulating, dispensing, and sharing valued tangibles and intangibles. Moreover, the resource that is being accumulated, dispensed, or shared is not always evident. This may make it difficult to detect the presence of the resource frame. Cooking a special meal for someone literally involves providing physical nourishment, but the diner probably views the experience through the deep metaphor resource lens of psychological sustenance.

9

Control

How the Sense of Mastery, Vulnerability,
and Well-Being Affects Consumer Thinking

Acquiring mastery over matters that affect us is a powerful motivation, and the extent to which we do or do not have that mastery greatly affects our sense of well-being. Thus, we become responsive to messages that say, "Have it your way," "Never let 'em see you sweat," and "Just do it."[1] These campaigns by Burger King, Gillette, and Nike, respectively, call on the theme of this chapter, *control*, a powerful viewing lens for consumers in a variety of situations in their lives—which may or may not include choosing fast food, using deodorant, or buying athletic shoes.

Consider what a global food products company discovered while developing a new breakfast beverage. The firm wanted to understand the role of food in consumers' early-morning experiences. Marketers anticipated considerable variation among consumers, especially across North America, Asia, and Europe, but they hoped consumers might also share important experiences that could inform global positioning and product development.

The company discovered that morning rituals give consumers a sense of control and that control serves as their viewing lens for thinking about morning food consumption. When consumers can perform their morning rituals, their day starts off right; they feel a sense of empowerment, agency, and efficacy. When something disrupts their morning rituals—if they sleep through the alarm, stall in a traffic jam, or encounter other events beyond their control—their day "starts on the wrong foot," and they feel "out of control the rest of the day." One consumer pictured a circus elephant balanced on a large ball: "The morning is all a delicate balance; the slightest deviation from my routine, and 'Bam!' I have lost control for the rest of the day." The image in figure I-8 (in color insert) illustrates how morning rituals lead to a well-controlled or chaotic start to the day.

Regardless of consumers' nationality, they viewed the consumption of various food products as adding to or subtracting from a person's control, sometimes offsetting the effects of other events on their sense of control. Although morning rituals differ from country to country, consumers worldwide used control as their predominant viewing lens. Using this insight, the firm developed one strong and consistent unifying global positioning for its new beverage, which is resonating well with consumers in all markets, even those beyond the regions studied.

The Origins of Control As a Deep Metaphor

Control is a powerful deep metaphor extending to all areas of life. According to cognitive developmental psychologist David

C. Geary, we have evolved with perceptual, cognitive, and affective systems that are largely unconscious and predispose us to enhance our ability to survive. He refers to these predispositions collectively as a "motivation to control":

> *There is a general consensus among clinical and research psychologists that humans have a basic motivation to achieve some level of control over relationships, events, and resources of significance in their lives . . . [The thesis] is that the human motivation to control is indeed an evolved disposition and is implicitly focused on attempts to control social relationships and the behavior of other people and to control the biological and physical resources that covary with survival.*[2]

The motivation to control extends well beyond survival needs.[3] It shapes our perceptions, judgments, and actions toward products and services that affect our own and others' well-being. We do not passively respond to offers to purchase insurance, hearing aids, vehicles with extra horsepower, stronger deodorants, or cell phone services promising fewer dropped calls. We actively seek and accept or reject these offers according to what we want to influence.

Consider a few everyday situations and expressions about too much or too little control with respect to oneself and others:

- *Feeling helpless:* "I feel impotent."

- *Losing control over resources:* "My spending is out of control."

- *Not mastering instructions:* "I do not have a handle on these procedures."

- *Losing direction in life:* "She is a ship without a rudder."

- *Losing emotional control:* "My emotions got the better of me."

- *Lacking willpower:* "He has no self discipline."

- *Lacking power at work:* "I am a little cog in a big wheel."

- *Obsessing over control:* "I am a control freak."

- *Demanding exclusive control:* "It is my way or the highway."

- *Wielding a superior position:* "He has the upper hand in this negotiation."

For many, the word *control* elicits negative images of powerful people dominating others. However, the deep metaphor of control works somewhat differently among consumers. It may entail influencing others, but it is essentially experienced as an ability to intervene effectively in life's events and choices. Control involves personal empowerment, confidence, and belief in one's ability to succeed.[4]

The deep metaphor of control is one that often works with other deep metaphors. We have already seen that control and balance are both called into play in shaping consumers' perception of breakfast foods and beverages in their morning rituals and experiences. The human control system monitors many situations, judges whether we have too much or too little control, and instigates change to align errant situations with a desired state, thereby maintaining balance.

Control and Emotions

Seeing your life or circumstances as out of control can be very painful. Across numerous studies, we have seen how consumers feel overwhelmed, unaided, and even abused by bankruptcy, bipolar disorder, incontinence, parenthood, and terminal cancer. If consumers feel a loss of control when dealing with a company, they may cast that company as malicious and exploitative, especially if they see it as a large, wealthy organization on which they depend; their sense of dependence makes for a sense of diminished control over an important aspect of their life. In a study of the automobile industry, one consumer used a picture of a rhinoceros to illustrate how consumers often view large companies in major industries: "You cannot get that big without being greedy at the consumer's expense." On the other hand, feeling in control after purchasing a product can provide great satisfaction: "This medication has given me my life back. I can go out without fear of embarrassment. I am in charge again."

Somewhat paradoxically, the control viewing lens also predisposes us to avoid what may threaten our sense of control or to interpret those threats as more benign than reality warrants. A smoker may avoid hearing about related health risks. Until recently, many people felt that global warming was a flawed theory or a threat in the distant future. That is why scare tactics and fear-provoking advertisements sometimes fail and why consumers sometimes ignore warning labels about product usage. We often know so much that we do not want to know more, a phenomenon called knowledge disavowal.[5] We unconsciously manipulate or control our exposure to available information so as not to have to behave or think differently.

Control, of course, is not an absolute with single meaning. Again, context matters and helps define the relevant emotions and type of control that consumers experience. For example, in one study, we found that some consumers overindulge in snack foods when they do not feel in control of their lives, thus producing feelings of guilt.[6] However, when those same consumers do feel in control of their lives, they continue to overindulge in snack foods as a self-reward and do not feel guilty about it. The experience of viewing oneself as in or out of control of life influences whether the consumption of snack foods is seen as a reward or a guilt-inducing experience.

Paradox regarding control is not uncommon. For instance, love-hate emotions surfaced in several DuPont studies about wearing hosiery. One consumer described the experience as "a jail sentence imposed by men." This reflects a widely shared feeling that hosiery is an imprisoning product, one worn because of someone else's wishes. More specifically, men, not women, are viewed as dictating the use of this product, at least indirectly. But many women, while objecting to the product, also shared the feelings expressed by this person: "When I have been housebound for a long time, like doing prison time, I want to live it up at night. Wearing hosiery makes me feel sexy and appealing. It seems silly, but it gives me a sense something good will happen that night." The paradox is that in one instance, the consumer felt men were exercising control by expecting her to wear hosiery, while in the other instance, the consumer felt she was the one exercising control—perhaps over men—by wearing hosiery.

Control and the Unpredictable

Some actions can put us in risky settings that make us anxious and activate the deep metaphor of control.[7] Some people actively seek out these situations and enjoy the rewards of managing them successfully. For example, a study of the physical and social ambiance of a gambling casino resort revealed that guests eagerly sought uncertainty—the reduction of control. Gamblers liked to "put their faith in lady luck." As one person said, "Luck is my magic wand, but since it does not work all the time, I am at its mercy." Interestingly, people simultaneously gave up control by trusting to luck, and exercised control by taking action to improve their luck. For example, gamblers might move from one physical space to another or strike up conversations with new people. The gamblers exercised control by changing the immediate environment, which they felt created a better, more optimistic emotional feeling, one promising a return of good luck. Some people felt that even the attributes of their hotel suites—numbers, locations—provided a positive emotional space where good luck could be renewed, thereby improving their gambling outcomes. Findings from this study were used to, among other things, reshape the slot floor layout from smaller, more isolated banks of slot machines to larger, more circular banks. By doing so, the arrangement facilitated social interaction between guests and made it easier for guests to switch between machines to "enhance" their luck.

Maneuvering a car at high speeds is another example of a sought-after, high-risk activity that prompts us to seek control. A study for a nonprofit organization concerned with drivers who enjoy speeding in their vehicles found that the feeling of being in control of the car's handling was very pronounced ("I am the puppeteer and the car is the puppet"). One driver, using a picture of a surgeon performing an operation, described the emotional feeling in control of the car: "You must know what you are doing and know how the car handles in all situations. When you are behind the wheel on a challenging road, you feel as if the car will do whatever you want, and you get a thrill. It is an extension of yourself." A leading European car manufacturer conducts consumer tests for car features such as the feel of steering systems and the company's advertising in terms of the message's ability to evoke feelings like those expressed in the quote.

Consider another car-related example provided by an ad for Pirelli tires. This ad displays a leather-gloved fist made up of tires on a dark, flat surface. The image of a fist both draws the eye and activates thoughts of power and grip, important themes expressing the deep metaphor of control. To reinforce and engage the metaphor, small print in one corner says, "Power is nothing without control." Control appears again in the fine print in another corner, equating Pirelli with "ultimate control." In evaluations of this ad, consumers grasped this idea even when no text was provided. Surface metaphors such as "I am the road master" and "I have a vise grip on the pavement" were used when consumers were asked to describe what the ad meant to them personally.

The visual image—of a fist constructed of tires—does an excellent job of communicating Pirelli's deep metaphor of control. In fact, control and power represent its basic positioning for the brand: Pirelli tires are high-performance equipment built to enhance the driving experience. This is reinforced by another deep metaphor in the image. The apparent wedding ring on the finger communicates Pirelli's association with the luxury car Jaguar. The association taps into the deep metaphor of connection. That is, Pirelli tires have a partnership or bond with Jaguar. Not lost on consumers is the message that their own connection with Pirelli will bring out the best in themselves as a driver, which furthers a sense of control for them. Jaguar becomes a stand-in for the consumer in the ad. As one consumer put it, "If it is good enough for Jaguar, it will serve me well, too."

Control and the Body

Consumers view many aspects of their physical well-being and functioning through the lens of control. We constantly monitor and attempt to control our weight, our state of cleanliness, our health, and how our bodies are perceived and experienced by others.

What We Ingest

Consider weight management and the role of various regimens that promise help in controlling weight, a topic introduced in our discussion of transformation. In one study about weight-loss products and programs, the frustrations of not being in control were very evident. In weight management, the promises of gaining control lead, paradoxically, to feelings of less control (and hence a diminished likelihood of achieving a desired transformation): "These products—the pills, the machines, the special meals—represent what I can do to lose weight and get a better body. But these ads really make me angry. They say, 'You can do it and we are here to make that possible.' My body is laughing at me saying, 'I have got a mind of my own, and no, you cannot do it.'"

Various products such as hard candies are resources that provide oral gratification. These resources give consumers a sense of control by assuaging their temptation to put a cigarette or foods even less healthy than candy into their mouth. As discussed earlier, hard candies such as breath mints are resources for mental control. Referring to a picture of a camera, one person explained, "Sucking on these candies is like a zoom lens;

I go from being unable to focus and being scattered to being focused and centered and able to concentrate. I would be back in charge."

What We Smell

Odors from our body, for better and for worse, say something about us. Consumers like to control that message. Odor control is the raison d'être for many products such as underarm deodorants, perfumes, and aftershave lotions as well as household cleaners, laundry products, floral services, sachets, scented candles, and other air fresheners. Odor control is also the goal of products that control malodor from certain medical problems, poor oral hygiene, and consuming certain foods and beverages. The control of these seemingly small "self-markers" provides a sense of control over one's life in general. One consumer in a study of body odor commented, "Control over your body is like control over my house. I decide what does and does not happen there. I keep my house as I want, very clean with a welcoming smell. That is how I try to keep my body."

In a study for a line of men's toiletries, the desire to influence others was quite pronounced. One consumer said, "When I smell right, as when I use my favorite soap, I feel as if I walk taller. I feel confident things will go my way." Another said, "I am convinced that the cologne I wear influences people I meet. Like a gentle magnet, it adds a little interest to me and draws people in." The firm is now evaluating the names of brands within a new line of products in terms of the names' positive control-related associations.

In a multination home-care study, consumers believed that the odors present in their homes revealed the character of the homeowner. Consumers both judged others and felt judged by others according to smells in a home. One consumer said, "When I first go into someone's house and it smells musty or of food when nothing is cooking, I feel the person lacks a good grip on life. She either does not care or cannot handle simple everyday chores. That is why I always have fresh flowers around my house, to cover up smells that only newcomers would notice." Another elaborated, "If they cannot control how their house smells, then they probably do not take care of how they smell. So when someone's kid is visiting and her clothes smell musty or of cigarettes, I know her parents must smell like that and are not really managing their life well."

Prosthetics

Many goods and services, when viewed through the lens of control, evoke the basic emotion of anticipation. Consumers look forward, usually eagerly, to something the product promises. When those product expectations are not met, the consumer is unpleasantly surprised. For example, a multicountry study of denture wearers found that the need to feel in control of oneself was as important as feeling comfortable, looking natural, and being accepted by others.

Feeling in control of oneself was especially important if one lacked control over the original dental problem. Some consumers described feeling that someone else caused their dental problems or that they did not have control over the treatment and care of their teeth during critical life stages. Some blamed a lack of available dental services, poverty, or a lack of insurance coverage. Others blamed parents and dentists who did not act responsibly and contributed to the quick decay and loss of their teeth: "He has on his white dentist outfit, is old, and has gray hair. Over a period of four or five years, he pulled nine of my teeth because they were soft and decayed. I think that my family accidentally put me in a position of having a dentist who did not know what else to do but yank my teeth."

Still, many consumers had come to realize that they did have more control over their teeth than they had previously thought: "Do not let what happened to me happen to you. Do a better job when you are younger, take care of your teeth, do not let some authority figure take over your life and make bad decisions for you."

Across all countries, denture-adhesive users spoke about having full control over themselves and their environments: "When I use an adhesive, I have no limits. I can do whatever I want." In contrast, nonusers of adhesives felt a lack of control over themselves and their environment and consequently felt trapped and inhibited in a variety of social settings, which caused them to miss out on life.

Health Care

Control is an active deep metaphor for many health issues. It is present as a viewing lens, for example, when patients and physicians discuss the treatment of bipolar disorder, cancer, erectile dysfunction, high cholesterol, smoking addiction, and infertility, to name a few. Diabetes, for example, affects many aspects of life. People often see diabetes as having "hijacked" their lives and preventing them from doing the things that make them unique. As one person put it, people with diabetes are "stripped of who they are." Another consumer commented, "I am no longer allowed to have the breads and the pastas that make this disease a death sentence for an Italian kid." Even the necessity of eating a different dinner from that of the rest of the family contributes to a sense of lost control. The sense of self is diminished: the disease "really makes me insignificant, sort of powerless." It is not surprising that the disease is seen as in control; giving orders and wreaking havoc "like a bull in a china shop—and I am the china shop." Many people describe diabetes as a vicious, malicious "enemy" that "beats them up" and an entity they must "struggle" with every day: "If I do not fight to control this disease, it will overwhelm me and then it will overwhelm my family." One consumer said, "I feel in a tug-of-war. Diabetes is pulling one end of the rope and I am on the other end. We are each seeking victory, pulling the other into our control." Using insights such as these has led one company to redesign its advertising for pain remedies. Simple descriptions of the product's efficacy had not been successful. Marketers added various cues to encourage consumers to "take charge" and abandon their attitudes of resignation about treating a diabetes-related pain problem.

Control in Daily Life

Overall life quality is often determined by perceptions of control present in daily activities. If a major highway is built in front of one's house, one will lose control over their home environment with noise, pollution, traffic, and so on. On the other hand, the smaller, individual moments of the day such as eating breakfast, paying bills, reading a magazine, or watching television are activities over which consumers usually do have control.

Several studies involving food products and their role in launching a typical day reveal how control interacts with other deep metaphors. For example, in an interview about the role of health food bars in his life, one consumer said, "You have not eaten for hours and can hear your stomach begging. You simply cannot focus on spreadsheets at a time like that! Yet you must because a deadline draws near, and there is no food in sight. Just as you realize how hungry you are, how late it is getting, and how much work you still have, your phone rings. You grab it and bark out a sharp 'What?!' when you do not know who is calling. You realize you have lost control." This person described losing emotional control because his body lacked the sustenance (resources) to maintain balance with respect to feelings of hunger.

For many, breakfast is a must-have resource to maintain general control throughout the day. For someone accustomed to eating a large breakfast, a day without that breakfast begins "out of whack," and as the day progresses, he or she can feel increasingly out of control because of an imbalance. A good breakfast for consumers like the one quoted above gives the "power and confidence to tackle whatever challenges come my way." Consumers believe that breakfast beverages, especially orange juice and coffee, provide the "balanced energy" needed for the day's activities, thereby giving consumers a sense of control for dealing with the demands of the day.

Control and journey are sometimes joined as viewing lenses. A study for a family-planning organization illustrates the mixing of control and journey and their relationship with life experiences, perceptions, and choices. The study addressed how perceptions of society, specific institutions, knowledge or lack of knowledge, and biology create pressures and restrictions that lead individuals to feeling out of control. At the same time, being able to make personal choices in the face of these restrictions provides a sense of control while one is embarking on a successful life journey. Expressions involving elements of both journey and control were common: "Be prepared for what lies ahead," "There are lots of paths that you can choose," "It is like a stepping-stone or a ladder to climb," "Go forward and try again to achieve goals," and "Knowledge is power." One interviewee, referring to a photo of a female artist, observed, "She was a woman artist who marched to her own drummer, did not marry, and made a career of her work. She did not bend to society's norms. Family-planning agencies give you that option. You need not have children. You could have as many relationships with men as you want. It is empowering to control that."

Technology and Media

Technology is meant to give humans more control, yet do computers and software systems give us more or less control over our daily life? Both, it turns out. The computer is a resource that frees up time and yet takes it away. One consumer in a study for a software provider expressed this duality as follows: "It lets me pay my bills faster and save time since I can work at home more often. But I go online, and before I know it, three hours have gone by, my husband has gone to bed, and I have missed my favorite TV program."

In addition, computers have a dark side that transcends simply getting entrapped or immersed in late-night Internet searches. Control becomes especially prominent with unpleasant surprises—computers crash, get viruses, bring unwarranted intrusions, and are implicated in identity theft. The person quoted above went on to comment: "I feel so vulnerable sometimes because I have become so dependent; it seems like the computer has the upper hand." Software is viewed as the tool that makes computers controllable. It helps consumers gain a sense of control by finding and manipulating information required to accomplish important personal and professional tasks and goals: "It puts people in the driver's seat. Sometimes I just feel like the engineer in the 'Little Train That Could' story."

How do consumers feel about looking at magazine advertisements in comparison with television ads? A Condé Nast Publications study explored how consumers frame their experiences.[8] Although the overall results support the use of both media as advertising channels, there arose an interesting container-oriented difference that comingled with control as a viewing lens. Consumers consistently spoke of "advertising *in* magazines" versus "advertising *on* television." They felt held or contained in a magazine ad and therefore more personally engaged than when they were watching an ad *on* TV: "Looking at the magazine ads feels like an embrace because you can look repeatedly," and "I could sometimes even get so far as to feel a picture and what it represents. Like luxurious cashmere, this sure feels good."

The differential consumer involvement with advertising in the two different sources was largely framed in terms of control. Magazines, in contrast to television, offer more control over the advertising experience. One consumer explained, "A magazine ad is like a glass of wine because I have the time to sniff it and appreciate it. I can take it or leave it. Because I have control, I can take time to decide which ads I will savor and absorb. This is so refreshing after seeing all the junk on TV." Another consumer said, "I have more control with TiVo, and so it resembles the magazine experience. The sound, representing television commercials, is a regimented march, as if they say: 'Eight minutes of the television have expired. Now you get to sit through a minute and a half or two minutes of commercials.' The sound of magazines would be lighthearted jazz, representing where your mind can go when you have more control over the experience."

Financial Investing

Another life experience in which control is a major theme is financial investing. Even when they feel confident about their investment choices, consumers worry that too many things beyond their control will affect the outcomes of their decisions. One person, referring to a segment of her digital image showing a person holding her head and crying, expressed the fear of losing control over investment outcomes: "When making investment decisions, I feel like covering my ears in agony. Not really crying yet, but saying, 'Oh my God, what have I done?' Even though I have a high level of confidence, how my decisions could impact my family terrifies me."

A consumer in another investment study, referring to a picture of a prison, likens not having control to being trapped: "I feel like a prisoner of circumstance. If you have money invested in real estate in New Orleans, you are a prisoner there. You have no control over that. The value of that industry will decline. It will be catastrophic if that is part of your financial plan."

Many people feel they lack the knowledge, skills, and even self-control to make wise investments on their own: "I could not force myself to attend the seminars even though they were free and would have helped me choose a financial adviser. But deep down, I knew I would never have the discipline to put money away. I am not a squirrel; I cannot squirrel away nuts. I would eat the nuts."

On the other hand, others do take control: "Before I took control and started investing and learning, I thought, 'The future will be OK.' But that is naive and silly thinking, because the future will not be OK unless you make it OK. So you must take control."

Sometimes this control is exercised vigorously and sometimes with timidity. These two quotes illustrate:

- "I am an entrepreneur who has many tools and is fascinated by tools and how he can use them. My investments are my projects and I use my tools to build a house for my investments. I am a fox and the fox is always in the hunt looking for opportunity."

- "Some of these people have lost their life savings. Dealing with investments is intimidating and could scare you completely out of the stock market. You can get hurt. I was confused, concerned, but again, I knew not to invest a lot of money, because I did not know exactly what I was doing."

Summary

The deep metaphor of control arises from a basic and largely unconscious motivation to control ourselves, others, and the situations we encounter. This motivation is activated by perceptual, cognitive, and affective systems that incline us to understand the objects and events in the world in terms of their impact on our well-being.

- Control influences and is influenced by our mind and body.

- Control influences our decisions to acquire various goods and services, or causes us to enact particular behaviors, all of which either add to or subtract from our sense of control.

- The deep metaphor of control often operates in conjunction with other deep metaphors, often balance and resource.

The concept of metaphors operating in conjunction with one another will help introduce the discussion of how deep metaphors blend, which is treated in the next chapter.

10

Deep Metaphors
at Work

A Strategy for Workable Wondering

We have introduced you to seven giants living in the land of Metaphoria. If you want to overcome the depth deficit prevalent in consumer marketing and evidenced by failed product launches, ineffective marketing communications, and me-too research and development, then you must learn to identify and engage these giants. As more managers are discovering, understanding the rich functioning of the unconscious can help you achieve your marketing goals, but you must also engage in deep, disciplined, and imaginative thinking or what we call workable wondering. This chapter shows how the disciplined use of deep metaphors contributes to workable wondering and underscores the fact that deep metaphors extend to all areas of life, not just commercial consumption.

Putting Deep Metaphors to Work

To become truly consumer-centric as a manager and as an organization, you must understand the deep metaphors consumers use when they are thinking about the goods and services that help them achieve their goals. We have shown how managers have used deep metaphors to accomplish numerous marketing tasks, including these:

- Segment markets more effectively

- Develop, execute, and evaluate advertising messages and campaigns

- Design more appealing buildings, office and retail environments, vehicles, jewelry, product packages, and point-of-purchase displays

- Develop new product ideas

- Position new products and reposition existing ones

What Managers Should Keep in Mind

As you begin listening for and using deep metaphors within your organization, keep in mind the following:

- *Methods do matter—up to a point.* Managers understandably prefer working with insights generated by familiar research methods with known trade-offs. Using a familiar but ill-fitting method is likely to yield impoverished and misleading insights. No amount of imagination can correct that. Choose the methods best suited to the nature of the problem.

- *Every research methodology involves trade-offs.* In the imaginative thinking process, any apparent consumer insight must be reliable and substantive and reflect deep unconscious (as well as conscious) consumer thoughts. Such insights can come from mathematical modeling, biometrics, in-depth interviews, observational techniques, or other sound methods, all of which are compromises with reality. Use multiple methods to understand an issue.

- *Workable wondering trumps research technique.* Once you develop a deep consumer insight, say, that social balance or physical transformation matters to consumers in a particular context, your management team's workable wondering counts more than the method you used to generate the insight, provided that your method was sound.

- *Data alone are just data.* Too often, managers mistakenly expect data to pronounce "answers," and sometimes the data do give answers when the research problem is simple and straightforward. But they rarely do when the problem is tough, messy, or ill-structured—and we all know that the solutions to these complex problems hold the key to a company's success. Do not mistake data for solutions, ideas, insights, or strategies. These are provided by how managers exercise their imagination.

- *There are no easy solutions, just prescriptions for failure.* When an answer immediately emerges from the data, the researchers probably rigged it into the study. That is, their confirmatory research mind-set unwittingly designed the study to arrive at the apparent solution. Beware of obvious conclusions.

- *Knowing the deep metaphor is not enough*. Effective workable wondering requires knowledge of the various deep metaphor themes involved, the associated emotions, and the type of cues that will likely activate a deep metaphor positively or negatively in a particular context. Once you have identified a particular deep metaphor operating as a viewing lens, use methods that uncover the rich texture of thoughts and feelings surrounding this deep metaphor. Probe more deeply around that metaphor.

- *A metaphor is just a metaphor*. The identification of a relevant deep metaphor, no matter the methodology used, does not alone constitute an answer to a tactical or strategic question. Rather, each deep metaphor presents options that managers can exercise imaginatively, as with any other consumer insight. Explore all your options.

- *Every manager thinks and sees differently*. Individual managers vary in their workable wondering skills and styles; not everyone imagines similarly or successfully. Some people and ideas fly, some flail. Different managers, bringing different backgrounds to bear, may develop somewhat different views of the same data or may apply the same insight differently. Therefore, we do not prescribe precise steps to follow in "thinking imaginatively." Celebrate and leverage these managerial differences.

A Sample Framework for Thinking Deeply

Figure 10-1 provides a basic framework to help managers think more deeply and go beyond product and service attributes and

FIGURE 10-1

Reaching customer values and goals

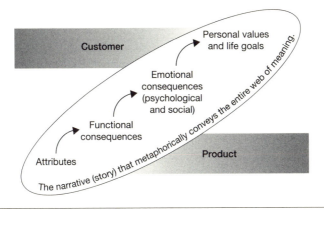

functional consequences (which matter, of course). Managers need to reach to deeper levels of thinking about (1) the psychological and social reasons why consumers care about those attributes and functional outcomes and, more deeply still, (2) how those reasons link to consumers' personal values and goals.

Surface, thematic, and deep metaphors help us link these increasingly deep levels of consumer and manager thinking. For example, Oticon, a large international hearing-aid manufacturer, wanted to understand consumers' thoughts and feelings not just about living with hearing loss and using hearing aids, but also about the deep emotional barriers that prevented so many people with significant hearing loss from seeking assistance. Previous research showed that approximately 80 percent of the "hearing impaired" refused to wear hearing aids, despite their health-care providers' recommendation. These potential customers often cited cost or inconvenience as excuses for not getting a hearing device. Nearly all industry communications focused on product attributes and functional benefits. The Oticon team believed that other factors, which were deeper, more important, and more difficult to express, were affecting consumers' decisions. In short, managers imagined a significant "say-mean" gap.

According to Oticon's research, consumers framed hearing loss and associated corrective products largely in container, connection, and transformation metaphors. The expressions revealed several social and psychological consequences of hearing loss and corrective devices. Managers knew some of these consequences, of course, but discovered important new insights into how consumers experienced hearing problems and how people experienced solutions to those problems relative to their own values and life goals. In describing their feelings about hearing aids, participants revealed that hearing aids were a glaring "neon sign" that the wearer was flawed. Younger consumers feared being seen as "retarded," while older participants feared being seen as "decrepit." Both groups felt that hearing devices conveyed deficiency, weakness, breakage, and ugliness—to them, the opposite qualities that society at large values. Ultimately, this overwhelming stigma and the associated fears discouraged consumers from reentering the normal hearing world with hearing aids.

What device, beyond one having technical superiority to current choices, could possibly appeal to these "highly resistant" consumers? Upon deep probing, consumers revealed a desire for a product that would transform them in two ways. First, they wanted to be transformed from a state of feeling and looking flawed to one in which they felt and looked closer to their ideal appearance. Second, and consequently, they wanted to move from a state of entrapment to "a whole new world" that differed radically from the negative world from which they initially retreated.

Armed with these deep insights and the metaphors that consumers themselves used when talking about hearing loss and hearing aids, Oticon worked with a version of figure 10-2 to position a new line of products. The technical superiority, design, and advertising of the new products all stemmed from a message of (1) escape from entrapment and (2) transformation from flawed to attractive. The shape and name of the new product,

Figure 10-2: Deep Metaphors in Communications

Delta, symbolize this transformation. The new devices are physically designed to look like high-tech communication devices
rather than traditional hearing aids. They are designed to be
small and discreet when worn, but to be attractive and colorful
when taken off and shown to others. Further product testing
confirmed that people did mistake the devices for something
other than a hearing device. One consumer told us, "This guy
asked me, 'Is that for your cell phone?' because he thought it
was an ear piece for a cell phone. I told him, 'Yes, it is.' He did
not think it was a hearing aid."

The advertisement for Delta in figure 10-2 shows an attrac-
tive-looking hearing aid escaping from a cage offering greater
freedom. Advertising testing revealed that this ad encouraged
consumers to create a story involving leaving a self-imposed
prison and entering normal social life. Testing showed that Oticon's use of the container frame also effectively engaged the
deep metaphors of connection and transformation found in the
initial research.

Note that the "solution" involved more than an effective advertising campaign. It also involved a significantly improved
technology as well as innovative product design. Oticon communicated how the improved product features and benefits had
social and psychological significance to consumers and how its
hearing aids fit with consumers' values and supported their important life goals.

A Guide to Choosing
the Right Deep Metaphor

When multiple deep metaphors are relevant to a topic, focus on
just one or two when developing a marketing strategy. The Oticon advertisement successfully stressed the container metaphor

while allowing consumers to add their own version of the other deep metaphors.[1]

Also, it is best to leverage one deep metaphor really well, rather than a few metaphors poorly. Attempting to engage too many deep metaphors explicitly at once can lead to confusing communications. Additionally, since deep metaphors often work together, activating one effectively is likely to prompt consumers to activate the other positive, related deep metaphors.

When choosing a metaphor or two to use as a strategic focus, ask questions like those below. We offer them in no special order, since their relevance varies depending on the strategic issue being addressed, the brand's history, its existing strengths and weaknesses, the source of its present equity, and the current and anticipated competitive environment—all of which should be known.

1. Which deep metaphors or which thematic expressions of them do competitors own, if any? How firmly do these companies own them? How much would you have to pay to capture ownership? Can you co-own? Budweiser beer owns a thematic expression of connection, and Michelin tires own the container metaphor. Winning the ownership of these deep metaphors would be costly for competitors, whose efforts would automatically and paradoxically cause consumers to think about their competitors.

2. Which deep metaphor works best with relevant consumer emotions? According to a Mind of the Market Lab study of candy bars, the Nestlé Crunch bar leverages the deep metaphor of connection—connection with self and with others—and the associated strong feelings of belonging and childhood memories. Consumers

used imagery of retreating into oneself and enjoying "quiet moments with just the candy bar for company" as well as the pleasure of sharing it with others.

3. Which deep metaphor will most likely activate other relevant deep metaphors? Are there natural overlaps that you can leverage, so that focusing on one particular deep metaphor will more certainly activate others? The Oticon case illustrates how the emphasis of one deep metaphor (container) automatically brings forth other deep metaphors (connection, transformation) naturally present when consumers think about hearing loss.

4. Does a particular deep metaphor have a negative connotation that could surface inadvertently? That is, might you elicit a negative facet of a deep metaphor even when featuring its positive side? How likely is that? As discussed earlier, one financial services institution correctly stressed the deep metaphor of resource, but unfortunately it unintentionally created the impression that it viewed clients as resources. The intended goal, of course, was to present the institution as a resource for clients. Consider unintended consequences.

5. Should your strategy begin with one deep metaphor and then over time emphasize another deep metaphor? For example, you might select an existing deep metaphor as a means of introducing consumers to a deep metaphor more appropriate for a radically new product. In this way, a newly reorganized and greatly expanded health maintenance organization is relaunching itself by leveraging the deep metaphor of connection. How-

ever, the organization seeks to own associations with transformation—which it cannot own now because of its competition and its own unique history. Its strategy, while stressing different themes associated with connection, is to introduce transformation themes gradually in its public communications and in the design of its physical spaces.

6. When introducing a new product, does a particular deep metaphor cannibalize one relevant for an existing product that your company offers? One food products firm had to consider this question when considering a newly acquired brand in the dairy products category. The new brand competed with an already-established company brand. One deep metaphor was the same for both brands, and one metaphor was unique to the new brand. The firm was able to reposition the recently purchased brand using the unique deep metaphor so that the new brand was more complementary than competitive with the first brand.

7. When more than one relevant deep metaphor is present, they will probably interact and create unique ideas called *blends*. What new ideas are likely to surface when the implementation of the chosen deep metaphor interacts with other deep metaphors? Are these blends positive? Negative? A major telecommunications company, for example, found that its use of connection and resource had a mixed effect. Connection activated thoughts about privacy, and resource activated thoughts about the power of technology. On further testing of its advertisements, the company found that among some

consumers, thoughts of privacy and power interacted to produce thoughts of security. Among other consumers, however, thoughts about privacy and power interacted to produce feelings of threat and loss of control over privacy. After learning which cues activated feelings of a threat to privacy, the firm altered its communications and avoided evoking the negative blend that involved a sense of threat.

This last question touches on a little-understood aspect of metaphors in general and deep metaphors in particular, namely, how all metaphors foster the emergence of new thoughts and feelings.

When the Seven Giants Overlap:
Conceptual Blending and Its Consequences

Deep metaphors pervade all aspects of everyone's life. For the sake of clarity, we have isolated particular deep metaphors throughout the book, but deep metaphors do not reside in silos. Two or more deep metaphors are almost always playing together in our minds. For instance, Oticon learned that hearing-impaired consumers simultaneously use container, connection, and transformation as viewing lenses.

How can this be? Think about an important conversation in which the viewing lens of one of your colleagues differed from yours. These differences do not necessarily clash; they may even complement one another. During your conversation, you each contributed specific thoughts that reflected your perspectives. But during your discussion, new thoughts arose. Some of these might have been new thoughts to both of you: thoughts born of synergy, like improvisational music. Others might have been those you had forgotten and would not have recalled without that conversation. The deep metaphors that consumers use complement one another much as you and your colleague did. Each deep metaphor is associated with specific thoughts that interact with other thoughts associated with other deep metaphors. Through this interaction, additional thoughts arise. This generative power of metaphors explains why they are so central to our thinking. Quite simply, when thoughts interact, they lead to new thoughts.

During her interview, Jenny, the new mother who was discussed earlier in the book, explained one of her pictures: "These butterflies in a jar, they show how I feel trapped and helpless sometimes because of having to do so many things for the new baby. There is little time to do anything else. It upsets me sometimes."

The interviewer asked Jenny whether she could say more about feeling upset. Jenny paused and then added, somewhat uncomfortably, "I feel guilty about getting upset, and shedding that guilty feeling takes effort." Her feelings of being both powerless (control) and trapped (container) caused Jenny also to feel upset (imbalance) and the deeper emotion of guilt. Again, different thoughts from different deep metaphors blend together to produce additional thoughts.

Jenny's thoughts illustrate *conceptual blending*, a fundamental process in human cognition. It occurs when two or more thoughts interact with one another to produce yet other thoughts.[2] Sometimes these thoughts are new, in that they were previously hidden until other thoughts combine to surface the hidden thought, as in Jenny's case. Sometimes these thoughts are quite new, in that we never had them before, consciously or unconsciously. The essence of thinking is the manipulation of information in our minds.³ This manipulation can elicit previously hidden thoughts or can bring forth brand new ideas.⁴ Deep metaphors are the organizing structures for these thoughts.

Conceptual blending can help or hinder marketing efforts. For example, a toy manufacturer with consumers like Jenny would not want to trigger feelings of guilt through its use of advertising cues involving container and control. The company might position a new product so that Jenny would see the toy as freeing her indirectly from distress and guilt.

By identifying the hidden thoughts and feelings that emerge from the interactions between different deep metaphors, marketers can identify previously undiscovered needs and develop better communications with consumers. Additionally, by understanding how marketing communications interact with existing consumer thoughts to form new thoughts, marketers can develop more effective communications, identify competitive positioning concepts, and generate new product ideas.

Conceptual blending is like mixing paint. Blending yellow and blue produces green, a third color, but a green that still contains the original yellow and blue pigmentations. Like colors, many blends of concepts are possible. Consider the following examples of conceptual blending.

Designing and Marketing Hybrid Luxury Cars

In a multicountry study of luxury-car drivers, consumers expressed their thoughts and feelings about hybrid cars. One participant's comments were fairly representative of the group:

A hybrid car should be easy and natural to use, yet have the latest features that make driving easy. You should not have to train and practice like a juggler to make driving look easy . . . Driving it should be like strong coffee, taking you from a dull, boring state to an alert state of mind . . . The car itself should be a safe place for my family but pleasing to the eye, not like an army tank.

This person expressed balance ("juggler"), transformation ("strong coffee"), and container ("safe place for my family"). In the context of the larger interview, these deep metaphors combine to create feelings of control, comfort, and confidence: "I am the driver. The car is my protector. But I am in charge. Like that juggler. I can handle all this fancy, powerful engineering with my eyes closed. I will not drop those glasses and trash the environment. They are safe. I am not polluting, not contributing to the downfall of our planet. That comforts and energizes me all at once. That is confidence."

The company devoted two days to gaining actionable insights from these consumer interviews. On the first day, managers integrated these findings with their other, more traditional research on luxury hybrid cars to develop a clear portrait of the mind of the market on the topic. Since thinking is like steeping tea—the longer it steeps in the pot, the stronger it gets, up to a point—the company held its second meeting a few days later.[5] All managers brought two images of what they wanted potential new-car buyers to imagine when considering the purchase of a luxury hybrid car. These visuals helped the managers address their differences of opinion so that they could focus their thinking on the most critical insights and action items necessary to achieve their desired outcome—to sell more cars.

The managers first prioritized their insights and ultimately decided that control—control over the vehicle itself and over environmental effects—was the deep metaphor to leverage even though it did not figure most prominently in their research. The associated theme of enabling the consumer to become the hero became the overarching guideline for designing both the vehicle and the marketing communications.

This course of action departed from the company's previous advertising (like much of the industry) of the car, which sometimes portrayed the firm's engineers and designers as heroes. The old portrayal led to an overemphasis on technical features and design elements rather than an emphasis on the car driver's more important needs for control, comfort, and confidence.

Developing Taglines and Market Positioning

Conceptual blending is not limited to deep metaphors; it influences how consumers make meaning from brand names, advertising, and slogans.[6] For example, an auto dealership tested two taglines: "We are here only for you," and "Where else are you first?" The dealership's advertising agency expected the first tagline to elicit the idea of respect for the car buyer, and the second to elicit the idea of quality service. But, through its testing, the dealership determined that when consumers mentally combined the phrases "We are here" and "only for you," their minds generated the idea of quality service. In the second tagline, consumers brought together "Where else" and "are you first?" to generate respect. And so the dealership opted to use the second tagline in its various communications.

In a multicountry study of consumers who engage in extreme sports, an apparel manufacturer sought reaction to a tagline that translates into "Free at last!" in English. In its concept testing, the company learned that this expression successfully activated two deep metaphors—connection and balance—which interacted with each other to create the desired message of comfort. The company identified these deep metaphors by examining underlying similarities among the varied nonliteral or figurative surface expressions and the visual images that people used to express the meaning of this phrase. For example, one person used a picture of two children holding hands in midair while bouncing on a trampoline to represent "having spontaneous fun with close friends who will not let you go overboard or do anything dangerous. That is a secure, comforting feeling." In this case, the ideas of connection ("close friends") and balance ("not go overboard") combined to produce the feelings of security and comfort even in potentially dangerous activities. The idea of physical security and comfort embedded in the "Free at last!" slogan has positively carried over to consumer perceptions of the firm's line of athletic wear for demanding sports activities.

More Than Just About Consumers

While we have stressed using deep metaphors to understand consumers and shape marketing strategy, you can apply metaphors beyond the world of consumption. Understanding deep metaphors will give you enormous potential to improve the general quality of life. Consider the following areas of interest.

Political Conflict

If you know that people who are openly antagonistic to one another might share similar frames, then you can help bring them

together or at least help them find common ground for toler-
ance. Recently, at a public debate, a leading pacifist and a well-
known military leader "debated" their country's future. Soon
the opponents discovered they shared two deep metaphors when
thinking about that future: journey and balance. The speakers
also discovered similarities in how each other thought about
the country's preferred journey or direction and the leadership's
need to make difficult trade-offs when allocating resources to
achieve these goals. The pacifist and the military leader differed
in several other respects, but knowing they shared two important premises facilitated a more constructive discussion of
their differences. In fact, they reached agreement on some initial differences that neither had anticipated when the conversation began.

The Health-Care Debate

With a particularly heated topic, leaders must often identify
and understand a possible clash of deep metaphors. Throughout this book, we have provided a number of health-care examples. Here, we examine a nonprofit health education agency's
efforts to improve physician-patient communications. The
agency found that physicians and other health-care providers
view themselves and their prescriptions as a central resource for
preventing, managing, and curing illnesses. While many patients share this view, many others ignore medical advice and
discontinue their medications prematurely or do not even fill
them. Why? Because patients view health professionals and
medications not as resources but as unconscious reminders of
their bodies as imbalanced and flawed containers. These viewing lenses activated another deep metaphor—the concept that

the ideal, particularly the dark or negative side of ideal—was faulty. The notion of being flawed encourages the denial of a problem or its severity. Paradoxically, patients who see themselves as faulty see little value in medical resources. Changing this frame is a major challenge that involves deeply held, unarticulated beliefs of what it means to be unhealthy: every time one takes a pill, one remembers one's unhealthy or flawed condition and feels threatened. Even consciously understanding that physicians and medications are a resource does not overcome the emotional threat of being physically or mentally compromised.

The Decision-Making Frames of Policy Makers

In a recent study for a major foundation concerned with health disparities, we interviewed senior policy makers who worked for a wide array of federal agencies, policy institutes, and elected politicians. We discovered not merely different interpretations of commonly held deep metaphors, but also disparities in how the two groups viewed American society and the inequality of health through entirely different metaphoric lenses.

One group of policy makers viewed American society as a complex and interconnected system of individuals, institutions, and even ideals. Seemingly different populations and life factors—such as the overconsumption of unnecessary medical procedures by the wealthy and the presence of mold in old, urban housing—united in a whole. Importantly, viewing society as a complex system implies that the actions of any agent can eventually affect everyone and everything else. So the cosmetic procedures that a wealthy woman with health insurance elects will eventually drive up premiums for the poor woman who needs asthma medication for her child, whose condition is worsening due to mold. To address health disparities between popula-tions, then, one must look at multiple environmental, social, cultural, and biological factors rather than addressing a single issue such as lack of health insurance.

Interestingly, this group held a competing deep metaphor: the container of poverty. Leaders spoke of people's being "stuck in holes" and needing policy makers to "pull them out." This con-tainer constituted a barrier that prevented poor populations from fully participating in the larger American social system. While policy makers saw disadvantaged groups as blocked out of the larger social system, the disadvantaged were also necessarily part of the overarching, interconnected society. Consequently, feelings of anger and frustration emerged from the leaders' view that the existence of these two competing frames within American society will, over time, damage the viability of the country as a whole.

A different group of policy makers saw individuals as lack-ing the resources to progress on a journey toward good health and not as part of a complex system. The primary resources are money and knowledge, the latter of which comes from parental role models. As a society, we must balance our responsibility to provide public aid to disadvantaged groups with each individ-ual's responsibility for making good choices on his or her own and the family's health journey. This group also saw American society as on a journey, often described as an evolutionary jour-ney, whereby technological advances and the overall growth of the country's resources continually raise the level of what we judge an acceptable minimum health status.

The second group was also very conscious of America's lim-ited resources. There is only so much money and so many ser-vices that the government can provide. Beyond that, to create equal levels of health, we would have to take resources from successful members of society—who by luck, hard work, and better choices have traveled toward high levels of health—and reallocate them to the poor. The group viewed this concept as both unjust and futile, since all individuals in a society as large as ours can never have the same health status.

What Does It Mean to Be Muslim?

A recent study of students' thoughts and feelings about someone who is Muslim revealed connection and force as the deep metaphors structuring both the overall positive and sometimes negative associations about Muslims. These metaphors held for both Muslim and non-Muslim students.

Connection was the overriding deep metaphor. On the positive side, students recognized that shared religious traditions connected individuals and included them in a global community with similar beliefs and values. A number of Muslim students talked about daily prayer and how "everyone's touching their heads to the ground at the same time" fosters a sense of unity. Similarly, they emphasized the cultural importance of close ties to family and friends, expressed through images of camaraderie. On the other hand, distinct feelings of disconnection involving Muslims also emerged. Disconnects between men and women, religious elites and common citizens, and even Muslim and non-Muslim countries created a sense of unease. Emblematic of the duality of the connection metaphor was one student's use of an image of people sharing a meal together but pointed to a curtain that separated unseen women in the kitchen from men laughing and eating together.

The deep metaphors of container and force underlay many negative ideas about Muslims. Muslim and non-Muslim students alike brought in images such as jails to convey feelings of being trapped or restricted. Some students talked about the "closed society" that the word *Muslim* connoted to them, pointing out people who, in their view, were "trapped and silenced by govern- ments and media." Many suggested that Islamic countries wanted to insulate and protect themselves from Western influ- ence, metaphorically strengthening the walls of their defensive container. Forces—such as repressive governments that "impose on" populations or pressures from within the culture itself to resist Western influence—kept Muslims within this contained culture.

Personnel Clash of the Titans

In an industrial products firm, two key senior executives contin- ually butted heads with one another, because of each one's ap- parent unwillingness to change his position on various issues central to the company's goals. The firm hired a consultant to in- tervene. This outsider noted the deep metaphors inherent in each executive's descriptions of himself and the other person. For example, when describing each other, the senior executives used expressions such as "acting like a turtle pulling into its shell," "erecting a fortress," "putting on mental noise blockers," "going into a bomb shelter," "as easy to engage as a porcupine," and "about as open as a bank vault after hours." Such phrases describe the defenses of an unyielding state of mind. Although neither person used the term *container*, each perceived the other as placing himself mentally in a protective container, here a mental state that keeps one man's ideas in and the other's ideas out.

Interestingly, both executives described themselves in very similar terms—"like a sponge" when encountering new ideas and "as curious as cats"—and saw challenges to their thinking as "firecrackers for improvement." Both executives considered themselves a "gardener" in cultivating ideas. These phrases also describe the mind as a container, but a very different kind of container: open, roomy, flexible, and even welcoming. The consultant used these differing views of a mind as a container (and the knowledge of each person's holding the same views of his own and his colleague's minds) to greatly improve the subsequent interactions between these two key senior executives. The increased awareness of their automatic responses to ideas coming from the other executive (and others in the company) led to much more open and productive exchanges.

Creative Issues and Societal Problems

In our work, we have identified relevant deep metaphors and their impact on many facets of life:

- How managers approach ill-structured or messy problems

- Artists' and musicians' approach to their work

- Children's experience of being labeled with a particular illness or a learning disability

- How screen writers develop their scripts

- Homeless people's view of shelters

- How factory workers experience diversity issues in the workplace

- How coaches see their role in developing moral values among youth

Clearly, deep metaphors pervade every corner of life. As managers, artists, and other everyday leaders become adept at reading the metaphors that people employ to express their conscious and unconscious thoughts, a new dimension of human understanding is opened.

Summary

We trust this book has provided readers with helpful information about a set of universal viewing lenses called deep metaphors, companions to other globally shared orientations to life such as primary emotions, basic needs, and core values. Deep metaphors enable a relatively new way to think about consumers. Just acknowledging the existence of deep metaphors is a major step forward. We hope this book will inspire you to think more deeply, meaningfully, and imaginatively when developing and presenting goods and services that consumers will value highly. In this chapter, we have addressed several considerations in using deep metaphors strategically. Putting these insights to work does not differ from putting into action other kinds of insights developed using other methods. While the examples in this book have largely come from our particular brand of research, there are many ways to listen for, identify, and understand deep metaphors.

We also discussed the importance of conceptual blending or what occurs when two or more thoughts interact. Marketers must recognize the emergence of new thoughts and feelings and their associated deep metaphors (1) to understand what consumers mean by what they say and (2) to facilitate the development of enduring and personally relevant stories about brands by consumers, be it through marketing communications, new product development, or other means.

As we have pointed out, deep metaphors populate every aspect of human life. In this sense, this book is about the reader in a very personal, all-encompassing way. It is about more than just the consumers most readers are attempting to understand and influence. *Marketing Metaphoria* reveals the universal viewing lenses that we human beings employ everywhere, every day, regardless of our nationality, ethnicity, language, or other differences.

Notes

Introduction

1. For example, a recent survey by the Association of National Advertisers found that 70 percent of all executives among leading advertisers believe that obtaining and using an in-depth understanding of their target audience was the single most important skill set lacking in their firms. Another study in 2006 by the Institute for the Study of Business Markets, Penn State University, conducted among sixty leading business marketers reported that the number one priority for business marketers is understanding customer needs and what customers really value.

2. Emily Eakin, "Penetrating the Mind by Metaphor," *New York Times*, 23 February 2002; and personal communication with P&G executive, March 2004.

3. Other genetically encoded skill sets include notions of how objects can be manipulated, how forms of life work, numbers, geographical maps, danger, and what constitutes edible foods; the ability to monitor physical well-being; a sense of justice; mate selection; and many others.

4. David J. Linden, *The Accidental Mind: How Brain Evolution Has Given Us Love, Memory, Dreams, and God* (Cambridge, MA: Harvard University Press, 2007).

5. Zoltán Kövecses, *Metaphor in Culture: Universality and Variation* (New York: Cambridge University Press, 2005); Donald Brown, *Human Universals* (New York: McGraw-Hill, 1991).

6. Some of the scientific foundations for these steps can be found in Gerald Zaltman, "Rethinking Market Research: Putting People Back In," *Journal of Marketing Research* 34 (November 1997): 424–437; and Gerald Zaltman, *How Customers Think* (Boston: Harvard Business School Press, 2003).

Chapter One

1. See also Lindsay Zaltman and Gerald Zaltman, "What Do 'Really Good' Managers and 'Really Good' Researchers Want of One Another?" in *The Handbook of Marketing Research: Uses, Misuses, and Future Advances*, ed. Rajiv Grover and Marco Vriens (Thousand Oaks, CA: Sage Publications, 2006), 33-50.

2. Personal communication, September 2006.

3. Stephen Haeckel, author and consultant, personal communication, March 2007.

4. For an excellent treatment of emotions in terms of rewards and punishments and their role in decision making, see Edmund T. Rolls, *Emotions Explained* (Oxford: Oxford University Press, 2005), especially 426-453.

5. Jerome Kagan, *An Argument for Mind* (New Haven, CT: Yale University Press, 2006), 82.

6. For more on the idea of cocreation, see Gerald Zaltman, *How Customers Think* (Boston: Harvard Business School Press, 2003), 211-233. The firm in this example used a modification of Zaltman Metaphor Elicitation Technique (ZMET) to understand the cocreation process and to identify the particular emotions each advertisement generated.

7. Measurement abilities can sometimes lead us astray. Here's an example. A food products firm identified nine consumer groups for the breakfast cereal category. The profile for each group involved differences with respect to how rushed people typically were at breakfast time, ethnicity, gender, age, type of cereal preferred (hot, cold, texture, ingredients), how often they ate cereal at breakfast in the typical week, the importance of taste, and so on. The company chose to target five of these segments with differentiated products, packaging, communications, and even distribution strategies. The cost of the five programs was not small and included the cost of having different personnel assigned to each sub brand. After a change in management, the firm took a very different approach. The new executive first asked what, if anything, the nine original segments had in common that might be important. The answer was quite interesting. By studying the stories people told about breakfast cereals, the firm uncovered two basic ideas that were very important to nearly all cereal consumers. The firm developed an entirely new marketing strategy that focused on just these two themes. The new themes led to advertising that appealed to a much larger number of consumers and resonated with them at a more profound emotional level. The result was substantially increased sales and market share and reduced production, communication, and personnel costs.

8. Daniel Gilbert, *Stumbling on Happiness* (New York: Alfred A. Knopf, 2006), 229.

9. Elizabeth Spelke, quoted in Margaret Talbot, "The Baby Lab," *New Yorker*, 4 September 2006.

10. Don Schultz, *Marketing News*, October 2005; Zaltman, *How Customers Think*.

11. Useful summaries of some of these advances can be found in R. I. M. Dunbar and Louise Barrett, eds., *The Oxford Handbook of Evolutionary Psychology* (New York: Oxford Press, 2007); Evan Thompson, *Mind in Life: Biology, Phenomenology, and the Sciences of Mind* (Cambridge, MA: Belknap Press, 2007); and David J. Linden, *The Accidental Mind: How Brain Evolution Has Given Us Love, Memory, Dreams, and God* (Cambridge, MA: Belknap Press, 2007).

12. Drew Westen, *The Political Brain: The Role of Emotion in Deciding the Fate of the Nation* (New York: PublicAffairs, 2007), 329.

13. Steven Pinker, *The Stuff of Thought* (New York: Viking Press, 2007), 151.

14. Ap Dijksterhuis et al., "On Making the Right Choice: The Deliberation-Without-Attention Effect," *Science*, 17 February 2006, 1005-1007.

15. Zaltman and Zaltman, "'Really Good' Managers," 33-50.

16. For a related discussion, see Howard Gardner, *Five Minds for the Future* (Boston: Harvard Business School Press, 2006).

17. Manjit S. Yadav, Jaideep C. Prabhu, and Rajesh K. Chandy, "Managing the Future: CEO Attention and Innovation Outcomes," *Journal of Marketing* 71 (October 2007).

18. Jeffrey R. Immelt, "The HBR Interview: Growth As a Process," *Harvard Business Review*, June 2006, 69. Italics added.

19. Daniel M. Wegner, *The Illusion of Conscious Will* (Cambridge, MA: MIT Press, 2002); Benjamin Libet, *Mind Time: The Temporal Factor in Consciousness* (Cambridge, MA: Harvard University Press, 2004); Thompson, *Mind in Life*; Linden, *The Accidental Mind*.

20. There is an extensive literature on the discrepancy between stated and actual beliefs. For a good experiential introduction to this issue, see Project Implicit information Web page at www.implicit.harvard.edu.

21. For discussions of the importance of figurative, nonliteral language as a way of understanding thought and actions, see Herbert L. Colston and Albert N. Katz, eds., *Figurative Language Comprehension: Social and Cultural Influences* (Mahwah, NJ: Lawrence Erlbaum Associates, 2005); Sam Glucksberg, "The Psycholinguistics of Metaphor," *Trends in Cognitive Science* 7, no. 2 (February 2003): 92-97. See also Seana Coulson and Barbara Lewandowska-Tomaszczyk, eds., *The Literal and Nonliteral in Language and Thought* (Frankfurt: Peter Lang, 2005).

22. For a discussion of this point, see Zoltán Kövecses, *Metaphor in Culture: Universality and Variation* (Cambridge: Cambridge University Press, 2005).

23. Zoltán Kövecses, *Metaphor and Emotion: Language, Culture, and Body in Human Feeling* (Cambridge: Cambridge University Press, 2000), 191-192.

24. Frank Luntz, *Words That Work: It's Not What You Say, It's What People Hear* (New York: Hyperion, 2007).

Chapter Two

1. David C. Geary, *The Origin of Mind: Evolution of Brain, Cognition, and General Intelligence* (Washington, DC: American Psychological Association, 2005).

2. Gerald M. Edelman, *Second Nature: Brain Science and Human Knowledge* (New Haven, CT: Yale University Press, 2006), 103.

3. Paul Ekman and Wallace V. Firesen, *Unmasking the Face: A Guide to Recognizing Emotions from Facial Expressions* (Cambridge, MA: Malor Books, 2003).

4. Quoted in David Sonnenschein, *Sound Design: The Expressive Power of Music, Voice, and Sound Effects in Cinema* (Studio City, CA: Michael Weise Productions, 2001), 101.

5. Dedre Gentner, Keith J. Holyoak, and Boicho N. Kokinov, eds., *The Analogical Mind* (Cambridge, MA: MIT Press, 2001).

6. Margaret Mark and Carol S. Pearson, *The Hero and the Outlaw: Building Extraordinary Brands Through the Power of Archetypes* (New York: McGraw-Hill, 2001), 13.

7. Cecilie Rohwedder, "For a Delicate Sale, a Retailer Deploys 'Stocking Fellas,'" *Wall Street Journal*, 21 December 2006, 1.

8. Shaun Gallagher, *How the Body Shapes the Mind* (Oxford: Oxford University Press, 2005).

9. Edelman, *Second Nature*, 126–127.

10. George Day and Paul J. H. Shoemaker, *Peripheral Vision: Detecting the Weak Signals That Will Make or Break Your Company* (Boston: Harvard Business School Press, 2006); Max H. Bazerman and Michael D. Watkins, *Predictable Surprises: The Disasters You Should Have Seen Coming and How to Prevent Them* (Boston: Harvard Business School Press, 2004).

11. Jack Carew, personal communication.

12. Daniel J. Siegel, *The Developing Mind: Toward a Neurobiology of Interpersonal Experience* (New York: Guilford Press, 1999), 1 and 22.

13. Peter R. Huttenlocher, *Neural Plasticity* (Cambridge, MA: Harvard University Press, 2002).

14. See, for example, Jean-Pierre Changeux, *Neuoronal Man: The Biology of Mind* (Princeton, NJ: Princeton University Press, 1997).

15. Jerome Kagan and Nancy Snidman, *The Long Shadow of Temperament* (Cambridge, MA: Belknap Press, 2004).

16. Dinesh Sharma and Kurt W. Fischer, eds., *Socioemotional Development Across Cultures* (San Francisco: Jossey-Bass Publishers, 1998).

17. Edelman, *Second Nature*, 56.

18. Donald Brown, *Human Universals* (New York: McGraw-Hill, 1991).

19. Research personnel at several major corporations have independently conducted validation studies of Zaltman Metaphor Elicitation Technique (ZMET) with special attention to sample-size requirements. Every validation study determined that fewer than twelve people are needed to identify the relevant constructs and associated deep metaphors that apply to very large and often quite varied market segments.

Chapter Three

1. The biosocial bases for balance can be found in the following sources and many others: Pascal Boyer, *Religion Explained: The Evolutionary Origins of Religious Thought* (New York: Basic Books, 2002); Daniel C. Dennett, *Breaking the Spell: Religion As a Natural Phenomenon* (New York: Viking, 2006); Edmund T. Rolls, *Emotion Explained* (Oxford: Oxford University Press, 2005); Antonio Damasio, *The Feeling of What Happens: Body and Emotion in the Making of Consciousness* (New York: Harcourt, Brace, 1999); John Zeisel, *Inquiry by Design: Environment/Behavior/Neuroscience in Architecture, Interiors, Landscape and Planning* (New York: Norton and Company, 2006). See also several essays in Herbert Gintis et al., *Moral Sentiments and Material Interests: The Foundations of Cooperation in Economic Life* (Cambridge, MA: MIT Press, 2005); Michael Leyton, *Symmetry, Causality, Mind* (Cambridge, MA: MIT Press, 1992).

2. Shaun Gallagher, *How the Body Shapes the Mind* (Oxford: Oxford University Press, 2005). See also Robert Wright, *The Moral Animal: Why We Are the Way We Are; The New Science of Evolutionary Psychology* (New York: Vintage Press, 1994).

3. For example, see Heiner Muhlmann, *The Nature of Cultures: A Blueprint for a Theory of Culture Genetics* (New York: SpringerWein, 2006); Peter J. Richerson and Robert Boyd, *Not by Genes Alone: How Culture Transformed Human Evolution* (Chicago: University of Chicago Press, 2005); Peter J. Richerson and Robert Boyd, *The Nature of Cultures* (Chicago: University of Chicago Press, 2003); Pascal Boyer, *Religion Explained: The Evolutionary Origins of Religious Thought* (New York: Basic Books, 2001); Daniel C. Dennett, *Breaking the Spell: Religion As a Natural Phenomenon* (New York: Viking Press, 2006); Marc D. Hauser, *Moral Minds: How Nature Designed Our Universal Sense of Right and Wrong* (New York: HarperCollins, 2006). See also Wright, *The Moral Animal*.

4. This study was conducted in 2004 by the Mind of the Market Lab at the Harvard Business School.

5. Harrison G. Pope, Katharine A. Phillips, and Roberto Olivardia, *The Adonis Complex: The Secret Crisis of Male Body Obsession* (New York: Free Press, 2000).

6. Mihaly Csikszentmihalyi, *Flow: The Psychology of Optimal Experience* (New York: Harper and Row, 1990).

7. Herbert Gintis et al., "Moral Sentiments and Material Interests: Origins, Evidence, and Consequences," in *Moral Sentiments and Material Interests: The Foundations of Cooperation in Economic Life*, ed. Herbert Gintis et al. (Cambridge, MA: MIT Press, 2005), 3–39. For further discussion, see Richerson and Boyd, *The Nature of Cultures*; Muhlmann, *The Nature of Cultures: A Blueprint*; Richerson and Boyd, *Not by Genes Alone*; Robert Boyd and Peter J. Richerson, *The Origin and Evolution of Cultures* (New York: Oxford University Press, 2005).

8. See Ernst Feehr and Urs Ifschbacher, "The Economics of Strong Reciprocity," in *Moral Sentiments and Material Interests: The Foundations of Cooperation in Economic Life*, ed. Herbert Gintis et al. (Cambridge, MA: MIT Press, 2005), 152–191.

9. Hauser, *Moral Minds*, 357–358.

Chapter Four

1. Liz Green and Juliet Sharman-Burke, *The Mythic Journey: The Meaning of Myth As a Guide for Life* (New York: Simon and Schuster, 2000); Robert Coles, *The Call of Stories: Teaching and the Moral Imagination* (Boston: Houghton Mifflin, 1989).

2. Paul R. Lawrence and Nitin Nohria, *Driven: How Human Nature Shapes Our Choices* (San Francisco: Jossey-Bass, 2002).

3. See Vincent P. Barabba, *Surviving Transformation* (Oxford: Oxford University Press, 2004).

4. Chris Tilley et al., eds., *Handbook of Material Culture* (Thousand Oaks, CA: Sage Publishing, 2006); Sarah Irwin, *Reshaping Social Life* (London: Routledge, 2005).

5. For instance, see Eric R. Kandel, *In Search of Memory: The Emergence of a New Science of Mind* (New York: W. W. Norton, 2006); Kelly Lambert and Craig Howard Kinsley, *Clinical Neuroscience: The Neurobiological Foundations of Mental Health* (New York: Worth Publishers, 2005), especially chapters 5 and 8.

6. Irving Rein, Philip Kotler, and Ben Shields, *The Elusive Fan: Reinventing Sports in a Crowded Marketplace* (New York: McGraw Hill, 2006).

7. Olson Zaltman Associates, "Being Hispanic in America Today: The Voice of the Second Generation," 2004.

8. For contrasting perspectives, see Paul John Eakin, *How Our Lives Become Stories: Making Selves* (Ithaca, NY: Cornell University Press, 1999); Jerome Kagan and Nancy Snidman, *The Long Shadow of Temperament* (Cambridge, MA: Belknap Press, 2004); Jeffrey Prager, *Presenting the Past: Psychoanalysis and the Sociology of Misremembering* (Cambridge, MA: Harvard

University Press, 1998); Juan Carlos Gomez, *Apes, Monkeys, Children, and the Growth of Mind* (Cambridge, MA: Harvard University Press, 2004); Dinesh Sharma and Kurt W. Fischer, eds., *Socioemotional Development Across Cultures* (San Francisco: Jossey-Bass, 1998); Susan Harter, *The Construction of the Self: A Developmental Perspective* (New York: Guilford Press, 1999); Vittorio Cigoli, Eugenia Scabini, and Robert Emery, *Family Identity: Ties, Symbols, and Transitions* (New York: Lawrence Erlbaum Associates, 2006).

Chapter Five

1. Erik Kandel, *In Search of Memory: The Emergence of a New Science of Mind* (New York: W. W. Norton, 2006); Gerald M. Edelman, *The Remembered Present: A Biological Theory of Consciousness* (New York: Basic Books, 2001).

2. The topic of consciousness or the ability to be aware of being aware is one of the most examined topics in science and philosophy. It is marked by many different, often conflicting positions as to its origins and functioning. While conscious thoughts are very important, as it is in that state that they can be examined critically, virtually all thinking originates in the unconscious mind. For two excellent treatments of this topic, see Daniel M. Wegner, *The Illusion of Conscious Will* (Cambridge, MA: MIT Press, 2002); Benjamin Libet, *Mind Time: The Temporal Factor in Consciousness* (Cambridge, MA: Harvard University Press, 2004).

3. See Nicholas Humphrey, *Seeing Red: A Study in Consciousness* (Cambridge, MA: Harvard University Press, 2006).

4. These sites include the basal ganglia and the right parietal cortex.

5. Michael Leyton, *Symmetry, Causality, Mind* (Cambridge, MA: MIT Press, 1992).

6. George Lakoff and Mark Johnson, *Philosophy in the Flesh: The Embodied Mind and Its Challenge to Western Thought* (New York: HarperCollins, 1999).

7. Russell Belk, "Collectors and Collecting," in *Handbook of Material Culture*, ed. Chris Tilley et al. (Thousand Oaks, CA: Sage Publications, 2006), 534–545.

8. "De Beers Begins 'Journey' for New Diamond Style," *Wall Street Journal*, 21 August 2006, B3.

Chapter Six

1. Zoltán Kövecses, *Metaphor: A Practical Introduction* (New York: Oxford University Press, 2002); Raymond Gibbs Jr., *Embodiment and Cognitive Science* (New York: Cambridge University Press, 2006).

2. George Lakoff, "Multiple Selves: The Metaphorical Models of the Self Inherent in Our Conceptual System," paper presented at "The

Conceptual Self in Contest," conference of the Mellon Colloquium on the Self at the Emory Cognition Project, Emory University, Atlanta, 1992.

3. Mark Johnson, *The Body in the Mind: The Bodily Basis of Meaning, Imagination, and Reason* (Chicago: University of Chicago Press, 1987); Jean-Pierre Warnier, "Inside and Outside: Surfaces and Containers," in *Handbook of Material Culture*, ed. Chris Tilley et al. (Thousand Oaks, CA: Sage Publications, 2006), 186–197.

4. David Sonnenschein, *Sound Design: The Expressive Power of Music, Voice, and Sound Effects in Cinema* (Saline, MI: McNaughton and Gunn, 2001).

5. Gibbs, *Embodiment and Cognitive Science.*

6. David Howes, "Scent, Sound and Synaesthesia: Intersensoriality and Material Culture Theory," in *Handbook of Material Culture*, ed. Chris Tilley et al. (Thousand Oaks, CA: Sage Publications, 2006), 161–172.

7. Zoltán Kövecses, *Emotion Concepts* (New York: Springer-Verlag, 1990).

8. Paul Connerton, "Cultural Memory," in *Handbook of Material Culture*, ed. Chris Tilley et al. (Thousand Oaks, CA: Sage Publications, 2006), 315–324.

9. James L. McGaugh, *Memory and Emotion* (New York: Columbia University Press, 2003).

10. For an excellent treatment of this topic, see Lewis P. Carbone, *Clued In: How to Keep Customers Coming Back Again and Again* (New York: Financial Times Press, 2004).

11. Ibid.

12. Barbara Bender, "Place and Landscape," in *Handbook of Material Culture*, ed. Chris Tilley et al. (Thousand Oaks, CA: Sage Publications, 2006), 303–314.

13. John Rouse, "Fenway and Family Values," *Harvard Crimson*, 20 April 2000, online edition, www.thecrimson.com/article.aspx?ref=100590.

14. Jane Schneider, "Cloth and Clothing," in *Handbook of Material Culture*, ed. Chris Tilley et al. (Thousand Oaks, CA: Sage Publications, 2006), 203–220.

Chapter Seven

1. Robin Dunbar, *The Human Story: A New History of Mankind's Evolution* (London: Faber and Faber, 2004).

2. See, for example, Daniel C. Dennett, *Breaking the Spell: Religion As a Natural Phenomenon* (New York: Viking Press, 2006); Andrew Newberg and Mark Robert Waldman, *Why We Believe What We Believe: Uncovering Our Biological Need for Meaning, Spirituality, and Truth* (New York: Free Press, 2006); Dunbar, *The Human Story.* See also Robin Dunbar and Louise Barrett, eds., *Oxford Handbook of Evolutionary Psychology* (New York: Oxford University Press, 2007).

3. Leslie Brothers, *Friday's Footprint: How Society Shapes the Human Mind* (New York: Oxford University Press, 1997); Carolyn Saarni, "Socialization of Emotion," in *Handbook of Emotions*, ed. Michael Lewis and Jeannette M. Haviland (New York: Guilford Press, 203), 435-446; Batja Mesquita, "Emotions As Dynamic Cultural Phenomena," and Paul Rozin, "Introduction: Evolutionary and Cultural Perspectives on Affect," in *Handbook of Affective Sciences*, ed. Richard J. Davidson, Klaus R. Scherer, and H. Hill (New York: Oxford University Press, 2003), 871-890 and 839-851.

4. See, for example, Robin Dunbar, "On the Origin of the Human Mind," in *Evolution and the Human Mind: Modularity, Language, and Meta-Cognition*, ed. Peter Carruthers and Andrew Chamberlain (Cambridge: Cambridge University Press, 2000), 238-253; Peter J. Richerson and Robert Boyd, *Not by Genes Alone: How Culture Transformed Human Evolution* (Chicago: University of Chicago Press, 2005); Jerome Kagan, *An Argument for Mind* (New Haven, CT: Yale University Press, 2006).

5. David L. Linden, *The Accidental Mind: How Brain Evolution Has Given Us Love, Memory, Dreams, and God* (Cambridge, MA: Belknap Press, 2007), 103.

6. Naomi I. Eisenberger and M. D. Lieberman, "Why Rejection Hurts: A Common Neural Alarm System for Physical and Social Pain," *Trends in Cognitive Science* 8 (July 2004): 294-300.

7. For more on H.O.G., see www.harley-davidson.com/wcm/Content/Pages/HOG/HOG.jsp?locale=en_US&bmLocale=en_US.

Chapter Eight

1. Alan Barnard, ed., *Hunter-Gatherers in History, Archaeology and Anthropology* (Oxford: Berg, 2004).

2. David C. Geary, *The Origin of Mind Evolution of Brain, Cognition, and General Intelligence* (Washington, DC: American Psychological Association, 2005), 72-73.

3. Paul R. Lawrence and Nitin Nohria, *Driven: How Human Nature Shapes Our Choices* (San Francisco, Jossey-Bass, 2002).

4. Ibid.

5. Penelope Leach, "Starting Off Right," in *Child Honoring: How to Turn This World Around*, ed. Raffi Cavoukian and Sharna Olfman (Westport, CT: Praeger Publishers/Greenwood Publishing Group, 2006), 17-28.

6. Stephen M. Kosslyn, "On the Evolution of Human Motivation: The Role of Social Prosthetic Systems," in *Evolutionary Cognitive Neuroscience*, ed. S. M. Platek, T. K. Shackelford, and J. P. Keenan (Cambridge, MA: MIT Press, 2006), chapter 19.

7. Robert Wright, *The Moral Animal: Evolutionary Psychology and Everyday Life* (New York: Random House, 1994).

8. Margaret Mark and Carol S. Pearson, *The Hero and the Outlaw: Building Extraordinary Brands Through the Power of Archetypes* (New York: McGraw-Hill, 2001).

Chapter Nine

1. Burger King tagline, 1973; Gillette tagline, 1980s; Nike tagline, 1988.

2. David C. Geary, *The Origin of Mind Evolution of Brain, Cognition, and General Intelligence* (Washington, DC: American Psychological Association, 2005), 72 and 73.

3. See, for example, Kent A. McClelland and Thomas J. Fararo, eds., *Purpose, Meaning, and Action: Control Systems Theories in Sociology* (New York: Palgrave Macmillan, 2006).

4. For a broader, more sociological treatment of agency, see Susan P. Shapiro, "Agency Theory," in *Annual Review of Sociology* 31 (August 2005): 263–284.

5. Gerald Zaltman, "Knowledge Disavowal," in *Producing Useful Knowledge for Organizations*, ed. Ralph Kilmann et al. (New York: Praeger, 1983), 173–187.

6. For an interesting discussion of food and agency, see Judith Farquhar, "Food, Eating, and the Good Life," in *Handbook of Material Culture*, ed. Chris Tilley et al. (Thousand Oaks, CA: Sage Publications, 2006), 145–160.

7. George Loewenstein and Jennifer S. Lerner, "The Role of Affect in Decision Making," in *Handbook of Affective Sciences*, ed. Richard J. Davidson, Klaus R. Scherer, and H. Hill Goldsmith (New York: Oxford University Press, 2003), 619–642.

8. For a more complete discussion of this project, see Scott McDonald, *Through the Window of Neuroscience: A Comparison of Print Ads and TV Ads* (New York: Condé Nast, 2007). An excellent treatment of control and the future of paper can be found in William Powers, "Hamlet's Blackberry: Why Paper Is Eternal," discussion paper no. D-39, Joan Shorenstein Center on the Press, Politics and Public Policy, Harvard University, Boston, 2007.

Chapter Ten

1. Oticon verified the success of these ads through evaluative advertising testing using a modified ZMET technique to understand the advertisements' storytelling impact among consumers.

2. For a discussion of how new thoughts are created, see Gilles Fauconnier and Mark Turner, *The Way We Think: Conceptual Blending and the Mind's Hidden Complexities* (New York: Basic Books, 2002); Zoltán Kövecses, *Metaphor: A Practical Introduction* (New York: Oxford University Press, 2002);

Zoltán Kövecses, *Metaphor in Culture: Universality and Variation* (Cambridge: Cambridge University Press, 2005); Seana Coulson, *Semantic Leaps: Frame-Shifting and Conceptual Blending in Meaning Construction* (Cambridge: Cambridge University Press, 2001).

3. Stephen Kosslyn and Robin Rosenberg, *Fundamentals of Psychology in Context*, 3rd ed. (Boston: Allyn & Bacon, 2006), 347.

4. David J. Linden, *The Accidental Mind: How Brain Evolution Has Given Us Love, Memory, Dreams, and God* (Cambridge, MA: Belknap Press, 2007).

5. For a discussion of the neurological processes involved in the continued processing and integration of learning over time, see James L. McGaugh, *Memory and Emotion: The Making of Lasting Memories* (New York: Columbia University Press, 2003).

6. For more on this, see Coulson, *Semantic Leaps*; Fauconnier and Turner, *The Way We Think*, especially chapter 3; David Herman, ed., *Narrative Theory and the Cognitive Sciences* (Stanford, CA: CSLI Publications, 2003); Dedre Gentner et al., eds., *The Analogical Mind: Perspectives from Cognitive Science* (Cambridge, MA: MIT Press, 2001).

Acknowledgments

Where to begin? So many people have contributed in so many ways to our thinking that it is impossible to keep track of these influences. We apologize in advance for what are certain to be significant omissions. But let's start with the many firms, and their deep-thinking managers, who have allowed us to reference their ZMET projects in this book. Many of these examples are clearly identified, others are not, but in all cases they have added greatly to both the practical and intellectual richness of the book. Working with these managers has enhanced our own workable knowledge and workable wondering processes. We are also very grateful to the many companies, faculty, and students affiliated with Mind of the Market Lab—another major source of examples—which operated at the Harvard Business School until recently.

All of our colleagues at Olson Zaltman Associates, especially founding partner Jerry Olson, have been significant sources of insight and in many ways are invisible coauthors. In addition to Jerry, we want to thank a few other OZA colleagues by name: John Bell, Katja Bressette, Bergita Bugarija, Elizabeth Carger, Vanessa Cordova, Jennifer DiMase, James Forr, Josiah Foster,

Mary Beth Jowers, Cindy Koenig, Abigail Rendin, Amanda Smith, and Robert Ulishney. We also want to acknowledge the constructive input and global examples provided by our ZMET licensee-partners which include: Altuition (The Netherlands), Business Development Research Consultants (United Kingdom), CimaGroup (Chile, Argentina, Peru, Bolivia, Columbia, Venezuela, and Ecuador), Fortuna (Iceland), Frame Consulting (Mexico), Yoshinori Fujikawa of Hitosubashi University (Japan), Hakuhodo (Japan), IdeaLog (Singapore, Malaysia, and Vietnam), InnerViews (Canada), MarkQuest (Belgium), Mind-Roads (Brazil), Nordisk Media Analys (Sweden, Norway, Denmark, and Finland), Research & Research, Inc (South Korea), and TMRC Research (China).

Many others have contributed significantly by critiquing selected materials in this book. Six anonymous reviewers provided important critique and guidance that helped us sharpen our thinking. Additionally, we have received very insightful critique from Robert Barocci, Jack Carew, John Dymun, Dan Edwards, Giovanni Gavetti, Stephen Haeckel, Taddy Hall, Tony Kirton, Joe Plummer, Karen Propp, Rob Scalea, and Ann Zaltman. As noted earlier, we have reviewed many of the ideas in this book with insightful managers among our client organizations. While they are too numerous to mention by name, we owe a great debt to their challenges and guidance. We would be remiss if we did not point out the huge influence of many scholars and practitioners whose writings are cited throughout this book. These thought leaders represent a variety of disciplines of direct relevance to marketing and have greatly informed our own thinking.

A very special thank you is due our developmental editor, Kirsten Sandberg. Over the course of this journey, she has exemplified various archetypes including sage, guide, taskmaster, and caregiver. Her contributions have been invaluable.

Index